THE JAZZ WORKER

FROM THE ANTE BELLUM TO THE RENAISSANCE & BEYOND

A BLUES AESTHETIC

PHILOSOPHY

An African American Experience in the Development of Black Popular Culture

PHILOSOPHY (as a Blues Experience) of the African American during the Development of Black Popular Culture

Delridge La Veon Hunter

Teacher Education

VOLUME 3

A REVISION

BLUES AESTHETIC IS THE PHILOSOPHICAL UNDER PINNING OF AFRICAN AMERICAN REPRESENTATION OF ART MUSIC, LETTERS, DANCE, AND THEATRE AS EXPRESSIONS OF BEAUTY

ARPress
ILLUMINATING IDEAS.
EMPOWERING VOICES

ARPress LLC
45 Dan Road Suite 5
Canton MA 02021
Hotline: 1(888) 821-0229
Fax: 1(508) 545-7580

Ordering Information:
Quantity sales. Special discounts are available on quantity purchases by corporations, associations, and others. For details, contact the publisher at the address above.

Printed in the United States of America.

ISBN-13:	Softcover	979-8-89330-570-8
	Hardcover	979-8-89330-571-5
	eBook	979-8-89330-572-2

Library of Congress Control Number: 2024901506

Some personal thoughts about

Aesthetics

Brilliance

Original

Extraordinary

Best composition

Best arrangement

Best orchestration

Best performance

Greatest improvisation

Lovable

Beautiful

Wonderful

Applause

Standing ovation

Bravo!

Par excellence!

....

Thee jazz worker

The jazz worker is

Creative,

Thoughtful,

An observer,

A provider of musical ideas,

As one continuous thought

A student of sound that sings blue,

Make song into sound that rings true.

Seldom ever rewarded the money

Commensurate with the talent

IMPORTANT INFORMATION--- PLEASE READ

These groups of documents are written as a philosophical examination of the Blues Form as an Aesthetic. This is written to complement the other volumes on the growth and development of Black Popular Culture using Black Creative Music as the underpinning of this process. This book is divided into axioms and dialogues. The axioms are the actual basis of how Blues evolved as a Philosophical instrument. Once you begin to read, if you find yourself lost, you may want to read the axiom quoted, again. The three dialogues as plays are included to offer a creative way to look at the subject matter as each dialogue discusses the actual products of the Blues Form

Preface

When it was decided that the author would treat Blues as the metaphor for the study of the development and advancement of Blues Aesthetics of Black Popular Culture in particular and the culture of the United States in general, I wanted to have a sound basis in which to place my analysis. With blues one cannot go wrong. Why? It has chronicled the political economy of the United States of American since slavery. The analytic tool that has been used to inform this process is the Law of Position, a Position Theory. The Law of Position, a Position Theory is a paradigm that has as its basic premise, "we take as given the idea of distinction and the idea of indication, and that in order to make an indication we must make a distinction. We take therefore the form of distinction for the form." (G. Spencer- Brown)

The premise allowed the discourse to move the discussion forward by placing the characters in their respective positions based on each form of distinction. The important point for the discourse was to express the dynamic of the process. To do that we used the appropriate axioms in the position theory to see how this process was played out. The premise was used to examine social intercourse as a process that could be explained in terms of its dynamic interaction. Blues became the focal point of this interaction because it occupied the form most respected by social commentators and storytellers who employed lyrics with music to tell the story.

Since assuming the position of an icon of world popular culture, the Blues form has advanced through the different genres of music created applying the minor tones in composition. Giving social commentary by recording the events while they were in process is what made blues performers the lyric poets they were. The lyric poets were creative forces who infused culture with feedback on what was going on and what a particular people were doing that either advanced or retained the status quo. This idea of using blues reflection on experiences taking place everyday was to allow one to examine culture as a dynamic force with forms of distinction that had their own ways and means of informing and advancing the process. To examine the milieu of blues as it developed and grew since its introduction from Africa permitted one to look at the socio-cultural infusions that developed as a result of interaction between the African and European occupants.

It was during slavery the basic process of American culture was formed and set into motion. Current practices were invented and set into motion during these formative years of development. It is during this period and immediately following the War of Liberation that these formations began to take hold as processes that interacted with culture as it constantly reinvented itself. Blues was a most active participant-observer in this activity. The lyric poet served as the blues informant and was the carrier of culture's reflections that were constant re-inventions and reproductions of what was.

Blues was important because every time there was a social change, the music reflected that change. Look at every period of socio-economic change within the polity of culture, and one will notice a new genre in blues has been invented. It is with this in mind that the reader may want to approach the conversation that goes on inside the discourse with defined, i.e., fine tooth, reading.

As expressed at the beginning of the foreword, the discourse applies a paradigm called Law of Position, a Position Theory. This position theory was employed to offer guidance to the process of discovery as a reflection on that discovered. [See Appendix] The intent was to provide a deeper and more substantive understanding of our polity of culture. This occurred by employing the use of positions to explain the outcome. The asset of seeing processes as movements within positions, between positions, and any other combination of same permitted a search for more complex answers to past dynamics involving the social intercourse of people who were there as individuals yet were also there as automatic representative surrogates for the positions occupied when each entered the arena of discourse.

Portions of this volume also appear under Black Popular Culture, in "Culture of Whiteness vs. Black Popular Culture (Law of Position)" Book Surge, 2008.

Portions of this volume also appear under Black Popular Culture, in "Culture of Whiteness vs. Black Popular Culture (Law of Position)" Book Surge, 2008.

Table of Contents

1.
Statement #1, Axiom 4
When a name identifies each member as an equal within the form, any additional name assigned to that member indicates that within the form the additional name is given a different value.

Statement #1, Axiom 4
When a name identifies each member as an equal within the form, any additional name assigned to that member indicates that within the form the additional name assigns a different value to that name.

Statement #2, Axiom 4
Once the first form of distinction, e.g., "classical music", has been established and is accepted as the original and most favored position with a boundary surrounding it, a new form, e.g., blues, with a boundary is established as a separate form of distinction. The boundary of the new form establishes a position of inequality between forms.

Statement #3, Axiom 4
To create a form of distinction we must establish a boundary that separates the original as the first form of distinction from any other forms of distinction created thereafter. Once a boundary is established between these forms of distinction an inequality of value is assumed to exist between forms.

Statement #4, Axiom4
There must be a motive for one occupying the original position to offer names to other forms not considered part of the original form of distinction or of equal value thereof.

6.
Ugly Language
An anti-aesthetic practice of the most favored 13
Statement #5, Axiom 4
Once the first form of distinction has been established and is accepted as the original and most favored position with a boundary surrounding it, a new form with a boundary is established as a separate form of distinction. The boundary of the new form establishes a position of inequality between forms.

7.
Politics and Aesthetics 16
Statement #6, Axiom 3
When a particular is considered the most favored, i.e., that particular is determined to occupy the most favored position of distinction. The name that particular assumes can be taken to indicate the value of the particular because of the position of distinction it occupies.

8.
What is a Black Aesthetic? 17
Statement #7, Axiom 4
When a name identifies each member as an equal within the form, any additional name assigned to that member indicates that within the form the additional name assigns a different value to that name.

9.
What is Black Popular Culture? 19
Statement #8, Axiom 2
To assign a particular process value greater than others, different names can be taken to indicate the value of each of the process assigned . . . . .T   o call a process by the name assigned
indicates the value of the distinction assigned the process so named…Thus, to use that name to call this process again means the value is seen in the name called.

10.
Black Popular Culture. 20
Statement #9, Axiom 3
It is through the usage of symbols called words that we call the name of each boundary created to separate one form of distinction from another. It is through the usage of words that a language is developed to give name to the form of distinction.

11.
Black Creative Music. 22
What is its Relationship to Politics and/in Aesthetics Statement #10, Axiom 10
When the name of a cultural activity is indicated to express the value of that particular process the form of distinction is indicated by the name. In other words, the name is an indication of the degree of

value derived by and/or assigned to that form of distinction. Put differently, a particular culture thus indicated by an expression of the name is also an indication of the value assigned to that particular culture as a form of distinction.

Once a distinction is made for each particular as separate activity, one activity cannot reach the other formation without crossing the boundary that makes a distinction.

When a particular group activity is considered the most favored as a creative expression, i.e., the group that performs that activity occupies the most favored position of distinction among groups, the name the most favored group assumes, can be taken to indicate the value of the activity because of the position of distinction it occupies.

We take as given the idea of distinction and the idea of indication and that in order to make an indication you must create a distinction. We take therefore the form of distinction for the form.

When the name of a performance activity is indicated to express the creative value of the group that performs this activity the form of distinction is indicated by the name...In other words, the name is an indication of the degree of value derived by and/or assigned to performance as a form of distinction.

Once a distinction is made for each formation, groups on each side of the boundary, being distinct can be identified as different. There can be no distinction of groups without motive. There can be no motive unless these groups are thought to differ in value. The group that holds the Most Favored form of distinction is considered to hold the most value. The intent and/or desire of the Least Favored

It is through the usage of symbols called words that we establish language as a means of indication of the motive that brings about a form of distinction. It is through the usage of language that we establish how crossing a boundary of distinction is determined or when that crossing is permitted. It is the usage of language that the motive has as a basis of expression for a form of distinction that is made.

18.
The Applause Statement #17, Axiom 3
When the name of the group is indicated to express the value of the group the form of distinction is indicated by the name. In other words, the name is an indication of the degree of value derived by and/or assigned to that form of distinction.

A Basic Premise

We take as given the idea of distinction and the idea of indication, that in order to make an indication one must first make a distinction. We take therefore the form of distinction for the form. G. Spencer-Brown, 1979, Laws of Form, 1.

Part 1.

INTRODUCTION

Blues Aesthetics As A Philosophy of The Blues Form

The Jazz Worker examines Blues as an Aesthetic musical art form that operates with a philosophical base rooted in the cultural forms that have developed over the centuries of African progression and transplantation to the United States during the Middle Passage. The Jazz Worker uses Blues Aesthetics as a construct developed out of a desire to offer Blues on the same level playing field reserved for other musical forms from other traditions.

Using European Classical Music as an example, it is assumed that this form emanates out of the European fine art tradition. That is why it has been given the name "Classical Music". This name automatically gives one the idea that the music requires the listener to be prepared to create a mode of understanding where full attention is given. I have never heard anyone state that this music does not belong to or come from Europe.

Although the form is performed throughout the world no one makes that assumption. However, when one describes Jazz, the Black Creative Music, no attachment to the African American cultural form is considered necessary, except as an afterthought. It is assumed to belong to no one in particular, i.e., any number of cultures could have invented this Jazz "thang". (Ted Gioia) Everyone potentially owns it. This is the propaganda of proponents the Most Favored.

The work called the Jazz Worker takes issue with this assumption. With this understanding, the discourse takes time to develop a critical appreciation of the art form everybody calls Jazz. The premise here is that Blues is the parent of Jazz and, therefore, gives Jazz a foundation as a musical form that places it in the class of art music at its highest form. Blues Aesthetics offers an analytic appreciation of Blues as the underpinning of all new forms that emanate from Black Popular Culture.

Special attention is given to Jazz here because this form of Blues has assumed a tradition of improvisation that includes original and creatively arrived at compositions. The "songs" are designed so that one must improvise around the theme. Thus, Jazz, as an example, is a Blues form designed to operate within and expand the limitations of the music however the composer so desires.

Jazz is called Black Creative Music throughout the discourse in order to identify it as the creative driving force in the establishment of blues as the base of this aesthetic. In the discourse it will be alleged that it is through particular procedures applied throughout a given composition that the aesthetic is arrived at. It is through the advancement of Black Creative Music that Blues Aesthetics has derived its philosophical impact.

The actual activity Black Creative Musicians engage to bring about their end product is a production itself. As the artists begin to become comfortable with the instrument (inclusive) a spirit of invention evolves as the musical notes speak the equations in a manner that is fascinating, interesting, enjoyable, and exciting.

Blues Aesthetics: Black Creative Music (Jazz) as its Expression

The Jazz musicians make their decisions about what they are doing In the surrounding milieu though the use of performance music. Intellectually the performers, composers, and arrangers, are very attuned to what is happening in their environment. As musicians they have many environments to peruse. As observers, each has much to create from the things picked up. The process works because philosophically the creators are thoughtful beings of consciousness. What allows their Aesthetic to be Blue is the use of minor scales played to create tones that sound like someone telling a story, i.e., speaking to you.

To tell, a story, the minor scales are complemented by the major scales as they interact and intersect creatively with the each other. The performer plays with the minor scales (tones) in a manner whereby the music offers sounds with feelings, and emotion. These music expressions of emotion are created through the primary use of the minor scales to create tunes that are arranged in a manner that sound "blue," e.g. as "Kind of Blue" by Miles Davis or "Song For My Father" by Horace Silver make that clear. This "song" as a musical form is *layered as a philosophical brick placed there to inform the culture.*

With this understanding we refer to hu (her or him) as creators of Black Creative Music. The performer is present to impress the aficionado to want to hear what is coming next. Is the performer going to hold my attention with these expressions now introduced? Ahmad Jamal and Rangy Weston are great examples of this approach to the intro to/of the piece. It is either an intro to or an intro of the piece. Which ever, the listener better pay attention. Why? The philosophy imbedded in Black Creative Music is one of Improvisation. A "Solo" is now intended to be Improvisational. The aficionado is to listen, to hear. That requires a form of discipline. In return, the renderer must create an approach to that tune that lets everybody know that this performer has something to say and what is performed complements the others. How one builds the story is what determines what the audience considers original or unique. How one delivers this performance is as important as what composition is played.

The complement to improvisation is swing. The music is expected to swing. The Swing Solo serves as the form in which Improvisation originates. Solos allows the performer to do an either or. Either you perform a "Canned" solo every night or you learn to innovate the solo with something new. Louis Armstrong introduced the idea of improvising with his Hot Five and Hot Seven. It is Count Basis, Duke Ellington, and Fletcher Henderson that are the great producers of swing. Count Basic's "April In Paris" arrangement is an excellent presentation of how Swing sounds when presented as pure modern art. "Una Mas" by Kenny Durham offers another approach to how a group of artist may swing. Swing is about the execution being conducted a manner whereby the listener's body wants to move rhymaticly.

The ideal is to create such an infectious piece the aficionado wants to hear that tune again.Even if one cannot "dance" physically, the body allows the mind to take over the intent of the body. Swing for those who enjoy John Coltrane and Freddie Hubbard performing "Blue Train" assume an expansion of the concept called Swing. Cecil Taylor, Jimmy Guiffre and Charles Mingus all present yet another way the technique maybe exploited. Each one offers a challenge to the aficionado to "keep up." It is the Swing and Improvisation interacting as a Call <> Response operating in syncopation that makes Black Creative Music no longer performed by rote memorization. The improvisation comes about by one performer challenging the other performer to show the ability to improvise as uniquely as rendered by the prior solo. It is the feeling of being presumptuous that allows performers to experiment. This is Blues Aesthetic.

What makes the whole thing work is how the syncopation<>call<>response<>improvisation dynamic is performed as an integrated presentation. Integrating swing with call and response as a syncopated motion makes Black Creative Music as original art form. James Harris in 1744 pinned a three volumes treatise, one treated Aesthetics as the philosophical explanation or representation the arts. In one piece he states, "Music is an imperfect art".Recognition that a human creation Music is made beautiful by the imperfections the composer brings to the composition. Aware of this, Black Creative Musicians use these imperfections to innovate, discover, reinvent, and stumble onto, accident upon, a way and means of applying the intuitive gift to composing. Blues performers have always been aware of the pitfall of performing.Often a mistake in improvising has resulted in discovering something innovative. There is usually a quiet laughter after this "mistake" is played through to finish. The performer has to let the other musicians know a mistake was made. The response amazes the giver of the deed when it is heard "for real, I thought you did that on purpose, it was right on time".

Realizing that a mistake offers the performer possibilities of coming up with something original, Improvisation is now the norm. There is a method too these creations. The method is to make the instrument an extension of the person. By including the instrument in the composition process, the music may sound so fluid that it permits innovations unheard of in other forms. Mistakes tend to work better during the process of improvising.A mistake during the process of performing becomes part of the solo. Only the most learned may pick up the error. The other aficionados hear no mistake. They hear only originality. This originality is what makes it possible for Blues Form to operate according the philosophical premise that is the basis of what is expressed creatively while improvising.This originality allows the music to stand on its own merit. This is Blues Aesthetics.

Maybe we should define Swing here. Swing means to the song (music) has life, feeling, spirit, and depth. Swing does not have to be fast. "Kind of Blue" is not fast but it swings hard. "Blue Train" or"Una Mas" are not fast but each swings. Nina Samone's songs swing. Ella Fi

Black Creative Music is music composed, arranged and performs as art music. Black is not used here as a race color. Here it is a Position and Location as in chess. Black is the Least Favored Position and Location in an open society. As the Least Favored people they create Black Culture. Black Culture and Black Creative Music come from The Jazz Worker. The Jazz Worker comes from the Least Favored people in the U.S.A. All cultures, classes, ethnic groups, and genders can perform Black Music. The performers of Black Creative Music may come from these musicians regardless of mark of distinction.

The African off spring brought the minor scales with them from Africa. After being in the United States for a few generations the African became an American culturally. The music brought was adopted to reflect the new environment and the new culture. The music emanated from the three traditional minor tones of African. It was during the Ante Bellum that Black Popular Culture began to emerge. The Ante Bellum saw the growth and development of five genres of African American songs. While the process evolved Blues as a

2

form allowed many other genre to establish a foundation. Complementing the music a philosophy emerged. The philosophy was that of Black Popular Culture. Black Popular Culture allowed Blues to become Art Music commonly referred to as Jazz. Jazz as Black Creative Music created an Aesthetic. The process philosophically became Blues Aesthetics.

The African brought to the United States three traditional tones that were simplified into what W.C. Handy called "the Blues." The Blues, I simply call Blues, have evolved as a metaphor of world popular culture. As the metaphor, Blues has allowed popular culture to be assessed, stated and reflected in its fullest. Despite efforts to deny its relationship to and expression of Black Popular Culture, as a metaphor, the most favored from the Culture of Whiteness, to stymie its growth and development, Blues has infused world popular culture with the most dynamic music ever produced by humanity.

If this is so, why has it not been recognized? When those who are least favored are consciously promoted as such, their contributions are ignored, refuted. Or judged, i.e., reported, to be insignificant. With that negation, others who represent what the most favored would rather promote are rewarded as suppliers of the gift. Why would such a presentation of evidence be offered? To assure that the monopoly enjoyed will be retained by the Culture of Whiteness. In other words, Conscious promotion of members of the most favored is presented as composers of works they had no participation in doing. Fact of the matter is Ethiopians originated the music they claim ownership of in Africa. The Ethiopians invented three minor tones. They were the Ethiopian scale (Aeolian), Harmonic Minor scale (Phrygian) and Pentatonic scale.

Over the centuries, these tones and scales spread throughout the rest of Africa and Asia. It was during the era of the Middle Passage that Africans brought these tones to the Americas. It was in the United States that the "blue" tone had the people, circumstances, conditions and artists to evolve the sound into a world-class phenomenon. That development has catapulted the sound into a metaphor on all events and happenings experienced by the African people brought to the United States during the creation of this so-called "middle passage."

The enslavement of Africans was a turbulent activity catalogued through stories sang by the lyric poets of the period. W.C. Handy the famous composer of the newly discovered genre called this mode of storytelling "blues" with a "the" front. The word discovered is applied here because African American performed the form Handy popularized since d already they arrived on the shores of "New World." Good music thrives forever. The Americanized African tones opened doors for all to learn African music.

As the music grew, it expanded into numerous scales of the traditional minor tones from Africa. Most of this movement took place in the 20th century as the expansive nature of a music brought to the New World began to influence the dominant culture as early as the mid to late 19th century. As we can see most of the musicians that performed the music recorded by written score and lyrics during the 19th Century were of African Americans. After the War of 1860 had allowed discovery Northerners to migrate to South Carolina in 1862 as missionaries, there first discovery was African Americans had already set up schools.

They also discovered that these people had a large collection of songs both religious and secular. These singers consistently sang their compositions applying a switch between major/minor with the minor tone (sound) dominating a syncopated beat. The unfortunate thing is with the focus on recording, i. e., writing the score and lyrics, as a songbook of religious songs, little attention was given to songs performed outside of the church. In due time, the collectors discovered that there were other type songs sang outside the church. Realizing that the over emphasis on collecting only religious songs at the expense of other types created a vacuum.

3

In an attempt to correct this omission, an offer was made to publish another songbook exclusively containing these secular songs. Unfortunately, the populace showed no interest in these Devil Songs. The result was not until W.C. Handy published his works of Blues compositions followed by, "Father of the Blues:An Autobiography" did the secular music of African American become known. The exposure caused a desire for "Black music" on records. Bessie Smith became the most desired performer Operating as a lyric poet, the story teller would bell out her delivery as though this was the last supper you were a privy too.

These are the scales under which their performances were rendered.

The Minor Scale:

1. **Dorian.- C,D, Eb, F, G, A, Bb, C**

2. **Greek/Phrygian.- C, Db, Eb, F, G, Ab, Bb, C**

3. **Ethiopian-Aeolian.- C, D, Eb, F, G, Ab, Bb, C**

4. **Locrian.- C, Db, Eb, F, G#, Ab, Bb, C**

5. **Blues.- C, D, Eb, F, F#, G, A, Bb, C**

6. **Minor Pentatonic.- C, D, Eb, F, G, A, Bb, C**

7. **Harmonic Minor- C, D, Eb, F, G, A, Bb, C**

8. **Locrian Sharp- C, D natural, Eb, F, G#, Ab, Bb, C, half-diminished sharp, minor VII**

9. **Melodic Minor**
   Melodic Minor Scales overview (auxiliary notes in descending scale in parentheses) A: A, B, C, D, E, F# (F), G# (G), A A#/Bb: Bb, C, Db, Eb, F, G (Ab), A (Ab), Bb B: B, C#, D, E, F#, G# (G), A# (A), B C: C, D, Eb, F, G, A (Ab), B (Bb), C C#/ Db: C#, D#, E, F#, G#, A# (A), C (B), C# D: D, E, F, G, A, B (Bb), C# (C), D D#/Eb: D#, F, F#, G#, A#, C (B), D (C#), D# E: E, F#, G, A, B, C# (C), D# (D), E F: F, G, Ab, Bb, C, D (Db), E (Eb), F F#/Gb: F#, G#, A, B, C#, D# (D), F (E), F# G: G, A, Bb, C, D, E (Eb), F# (F), G G#/Ab: G#, A#, B, C#, D#, F (E), G (F#), G#Intervals and steps Intervals: 1, 2, 3, 4, 5, 6, 7 Semi-notes: 2 - 1 - 2 - 2 - 2 - 2 - 1 Formula: Whole, Half, Whole, Whole, Whole, Whole, Half

The Melodic Minor scales in musical notation are available in the member area. The scale in all keys can be downloaded as a PDF-file.

Any one of these keys or scales was recorded as the musical language of (for) the "slave" commentator, the lyric poet. All are minor scales. These are the same scales found in music from South-West, North-West, West, North Central across to the Horn of Africa until today. The same instruments that were brought over to the United States from these parts are played in Africa today. Remember people in bondage so-called "slaves" meaning "slav" in the United States came from every part of Africa. One thing that should be obvious therefore is the African brought this sound over to the Americas and never lost it, not even in the United States. All songs I have reviewed offer the basis of the blues as formulated today. Musicians of the United States south utilized one of the scales when performing one of their lyrics. As the songs in the text indicate all were of the blues motif in lyricism (content) structure (the manner in which the words were delivered), and musical (key, fluidity of instrumental use or form, i.e., the ability to stretch the AAB form as far as the creative will would allow). This ability has not changed.

Point of Information

There is a genre called Smooth Jazz that permits rote memorization. It is easy listening music. "Smooth Jazz" is studio produced. The performers appearing in public usually do minor canned improvisations on those tunes recorded. This is a genre separate and apart from Black Creative Music commonly called Jazz. Smooth appears to be more popular than Black Creative Music because it does not require the listener to really hear what is being performed by actually listening.

Tell The Story

By its name, Black Music is to be used as a case in point. Because it is easy to identify, its contributions to popular culture are omnipresent. A good example of how this might be is in the performance of Black Creative Music (Jazz). Before we move further we must explain what we intend to examine when we use the term Black Creative Music.

In this discourse the words Black and White are applied as positions and locations. As positions and locations they represent all people from the least favored to the most favored in a given society. Color here applies as it may be used in playing the game of chess. In other words, it's reference to color, as description of people is not in use here. All people are subject to occupy many positions and locations from the least favored to the most favored depending on the particular. Put differently do not mistaken black to mean "the color of ones skin." Here, black is used as a position and location as in chess.

Black Culture represents the cultural form that is identified as emanating within "popular culture". Popular culture contains the many forms that have represented what "common" people are said to invent, e.g., blues. Blues comes from the enslaved people who were brought to the United States from the continent of Africa. With them came a musical form that was performed with or without a vocalist, or, a vocalist without instrument. The music having its origin in Ethiopia, presents the Ethiopian scale as one of many minor tones that can be seen and heard throughout continent from Ethiopia through Mali to Congo/Angola. We call these scales the minor keys. As minor keys, how they are rendered, is determined by the presenter. The presenter is creator of the form and style of delivery. How the tones will be applied is left up to the lyric poet as a musician who has the desire to be heard delivering song by the means chosen by that composer. The philosophical form we apply to listening to the performance of this music is called "Blues Aesthetics."

5

2. Naming

Statement #1, Axiom 4

When a name identifies each member as an equal within the form, any additional name assigned to that member indicates that within the form the additional name assigns a different value to that name. (Repeat)

According to Kantian aesthetics, there is an assumption of equality, within the marketplace of art. There is a kind of purity that allows the artist and consumer to decide the aesthetic value of the piece of work under review. One may judge art on the merit of some assumptions agreed upon by the critical mass of an informed populace. However, within a polity of culture where the inequality principle operates, this does not appear to be the case: when one takes time to examine the marketplace of art of the consumer (inclusive), it becomes very apparent that art is not necessarily judged on merit. In this instance, we shall examine music as a way to see how an objective position of observation, whether visual or aural, allows aesthetics to inform the process; that is, the role aesthetics plays, if any, in permitting "good art" to receive appropriate recognition. The role of denial and non-recognition will serve as areas to review in our attempt to unravel art as a political tool in the process of recognition.

As a reference point, in our Law of Position, a position theory, "we take as given the idea of distinction and the idea of indication, and in order to make an indication we must first draw a distinction. We take therefore the form of distinction for the form. (Laws of Form, Spencer-Brown, 1) Thus, according to the Law of Position, a Position Theory, Axiom 4, the inequality principle is an operational form of distinction, i.e., a distinction is made between groups. A form of inequality is indicated by the name chosen to express the value assigned the particular form determined to be of less value. Once a value has been designated to that form by name, the name indicates the distinction in value attributed to the form so named. It goes further by stating, "There must be a motive for one occupying the original position to offer names to other forms not considered part of the original form of distinction…Once a name is chosen to indicate one form from another, motive has been established. The name assigned is supported by a definition and a value assigned to the name. A motive to distinguish one form from another by a name assigned a lesser value establishes an assumption of inequality between forms, e.g., fine Art vs. Folk Art (Axiom 4). Once a motive has been established the value assigned each form by the name called indicates that there is an assumed inequality between forms. In other words, all forms of equal distinction carry the same name. A different name assumes that there is difference of form. Thereby an unequal value attached to the name as a description of the form difference, establishes one called by that name as a position that is less favored than the most favored position. This describes a position of inequality of the Least Favored.

Naming

It is within the Basic Premise, Axioms 1, 2, 3 & 4, of Position Theory, that we shall examine the art called Blues as a form of Black Music and, as such, determine how it is governed by the rules of Blues Aesthetics. We shall examine the Blues form through its most artistic offspring, Jazz –so-called- in this discourse. Jazz or Black Creative Music (BCM) is chosen because it offers the best examples of how a particular polity of culture serves as the process that permits the most concrete manifestations of the interplay between Black Popular Culture and the culture of whiteness.

Question

Explain how naming works? Please, give examples using Jazz, the musical form as your example of where it emanates? How it looks?

3. Discovery

Statement # 2, Axiom 4

Once the first form of distinction, e.g., "classical music," has been established and is accepted as the original and most favored position with a boundary surrounding it, a new form with a boundary is established, e.g., blues, as a separate form of distinction. The boundary of the new form establishes a position of inequality between forms.

With the organization of slavery within the confines of the United States of America there was an ongoing struggle between the Least Favored and The Most Favored over how culture was to be prescribed. From its inception, attempts by representatives of the Most Favored Position were made to consciously destroy all of the cultural forms of the slave people as the Least Favored people.

This effort to destroy the African sensibilities was carried on so that all forms of cultural definitions would be lost. The Principle of Inequality served as the operational form of distinction that was indicated by The White Position. Referred to as the Most Favored Position, the White Position represents the culture of whiteness.

The white dynamic allowed it to claim ownership of what it did not invent, created or discovered and established copyright simply by applying the mark of distinction rule that states, "we take as given the idea of distinction and the idea of indication, and in order to make an indication we must draw a distinction. We therefore take the form of distinction for the form."

There are two forms of distinction: the Least Favored Position vis-à-vis the Most Favored Position. The authority invested in those who assumed the original position, thereby becoming the Most Favored People, allowed them to decide who would occupy as their nemesis the Least Favored Position.

The slave was assigned that position. [The Least Favored Position is Black as in chess.] There was no authority invested in the Least Favored Position except that which a slave was supposed to do, whatever that was. A slave's role was to obey the Master and his surrogates. This form of slavery was totalitarian where few areas of opportunity were available for use.

However, despite that the Most Favored's total authority and power was applied to destroy everything cultural. Despite the effort, a form of Black Culture was brought to the United States that remains, and sustains itself until this day. As a unique form of Black Culture, Devil Songs existed as an original lyrical form until "discovered" by Paul Lawrence Dunbar, W.E.B. Du Bois, Hart Wand and W.C. Handy. Today we know these, Devil (Sorrow) Songs as a form of music called Blues.

Blues became the most definitive cultural manifestation of blacks' survival of a virtual onslaught from the culture of whiteness. As Frantz Fanon's Black Skin, White Masks discourse on the struggle over the race/color mulatto, i.e., Creole, syndrome demonstrates, dialogically overtime the black skin complex became "the" obsession for (of) the Most Favored.

An obsession with keeping slavery as a means of production was complemented by a system of inequality forcefully enacted to assure that the African did not cause any more 6disturbance than before. Laws enacted made distinctions that were clearly indicated by the form as each position was assigned by name.

The motive for establishing a clear distinction was to assure that the African's place was well laid out and it was understood by everybody that these were the slaves and by the nature of this design they would occupy the Least Favored Position in society. The Principle of Inequality became operational as the mark of distinction. This form of distinction was indicated by the name Negro.

Question

When did the local public begin to hear Black Songs? When did the experts make their discovery?

4. Cultural Tyranny

Statement #3, Axiom 4

As a form of distinction we must establish a boundary that separates the original as the first form of distinction from any other forms of distinction created thereafter. Once a boundary is established between these forms. To create a form of distinction an inequality of value is assumed to exist between forms.

During slavery, ongoing efforts were made by the Most Favored to dehumanize the Least Favored people so that their efforts to oppose slavery would not face direct opposition. The people most feared were those enslaved artists who went about the community as carriers of the word through song and those whose humanity called them to oppose this institution with their lives. Respectful people called both "abolitionists".

However, the word "abolitionist" was assigned to the most favored position while the least favored were "black" abolitionists: not even within their own struggle for freedom could they assume authority of the position as "abolitionists" without the attachment of "black." Why? The Black was the Least Favored, referred to by the name Negro; Negro was the Portuguese use of a proper name for "black", it meant the same.

Negroes were the Least Favored because they were thought black in complexion as the children of Ham and Cain" The "color" black became "the Black" as the occupier of the Least Favored Position. As a Position, now, Black transcended color: it would apply to any of those whose distinctions indicated inequality. It applied anywhere there were least favored and most favored people.

Question

The people most feared were those enslaved artists who went about the community as carriers of the word through song and those whose humanity called them to oppose this institution with their lives.

10

5. A Sinful Case of Bad Faith

Statement #4, Axiom 4

There must be a motive for one occupying the original position to offer names to other forms not considered part of the original form of distinction or of equal value thereof.

Back to the story: Bad Faith existed when the most favored knew something was morally and ethically wrong but initiated conscious efforts to commit that wrong in order to deny the least favored people an ability to advance from their position. During the process of slavery, to control the least favored, the most favored outlawed manifestations of the cultural forms within slave practices that appeared to be too dangerous to the practices of slavery: playing ones percussion instrument was dangerous therefore, it must be outlawed; speaking in ones original tongue was prohibited, with a whipping forthcoming for such use of vernacular; worshipping in ones ancestral forms were called Devil worship, primitive, superstitious; and organizing meetings, reciting poems or singing lyrics that criticized unmercifully the master or members of his family and class were punishable by death. Such cultural forms, parent language, or mode of worship following the sacred texts, were immediately attacked and banned. The most apparent example of how serious the oppression was that, in most slave communities within the southern region of United States of America, the drum was a forbidden instrument because of the pre-telegram communication services it offered to the Least Favored.

To show how bias can blind reason, it never dawned on the Most Favored that they could take the drum, or an idea thereof, and create a "telegram" service for everybody long before the "telegram" was invented. The bias of non-recognition served to negate any effort to use the services of the slave beyond the capacity originally assigned.

No member of the Most Favored position believed that the African —who built the best houses in the South, who knew how to raise cotton, plant rice and grain, which had photographic memory of the plans to build Washington, D.C., and other inventions and discoveries— was a capable being. No acknowledgement or recognition of any possibility of intelligence was shown.

Put differently, when a member of the Least Favored invented something valuable to human and societal development, this invention was the assumed property of the most favored in that they could actually claim it as their invention because "Can't no nigger invent nothing." It is interesting how little if anything is ever mentioned about how this type of bias may have slowed the development of the South in terms of capital investment in communication and cultural awareness.

White bias would not allow a regional communication network designed and operated by Africans. How interesting that such a development would be comparable to the first canal built by slaves from Angola living in the Mid-Hudson Valley, New York State, connecting the Round Out on the Hudson River in Kingston, NY with the Delaware River near, Port Jarvis, NY.

A regional communication network might have increased commerce by providing immediate communication while leading to other commercial inventions by the least favored. No one ever thought about that because reason was placed aside when it came to slavery and culture. Extreme bias acted as a disincentive to progress in the very region that suffered from a lack of growth and development because it stifled creative ideas regarding social intercourse.

The previous example is only one of many major errors committed by the exclusion of the participation of the least favored that resulted from the cultural bias of the most favored.

Question

When is a sinful case of Bad Faith operational?

6. Ugly Language

An anti-aesthetic practice of the most favored

Statement #5, Axiom 4

Once the first form of distinction has been established and is accepted as the original and most favored position with a boundary surrounding it, a new form with a boundary is established as a separate form of distinction. The boundary of the new form establishes a position of inequality between forms.

The investment in the slave as human capital employed as labor, failed to materialize into an economic advantage for the south. Their obsession with "bodies, black bodies" is only one of many poor judgment calls made in the polity called southern culture.

As it turns out, the political, religious, social and cultural opposition gendered to remove black culture from the arena of civilization served to keep the art form we are going to around the Big House, inadvertently and/or deliberately did not inform their masters about the "bad" things going on within the community.

To tell about these things would cause the most favored to think less of these tattle-tales. What we find was these 'kept' strivers, in the slave communities, suffered from their own triple life: one life for the master, one for the slave and another for self. They wanted to receive as much fairness, called privilege, as that bestowed upon the members of the most favored, so they often lived a shadow life. What was a shadow life?

That was, when a member of the least favored acted like a "wanna be," so they did what they must do to stay within the favor of the Master Class in the Big House. As their complement, they lived in the shadow of the Big House.

They were the tattle-tales, i.e., the slaves who operated within the buffer strata: that group of the affluent-poor who are "middle class" in orientation and house servants in position. The tattletale buffer strata slaves wanted to avoid trouble as much as they could. One-way was to tell Misses all about what was happening within the slave community without ever giving away the secrets. Playing the role as tattletale of the buffer strata was not always easy. This was how it worked: well, no one mentions the "Hoo Doo" Priest and "Devil" singers except in the language that allowed the master to assume he knew what he really did not know. What did his family not know? They did not know that Black Popular Culture in the form of Blues was being developed right there on their "plantation." Nor did they know that this music would become the base and blueprint of American popular culture and creative music. He knew nothing about the black culture in the society in which he ruled, so he had no idea that what was being invented and invested within the slave communities where he it made suffering a focal point.

13

It was within the suffering that these so-called "sorrow songs", called escapist songs by the bondsmen,materialized through the lyrics and music style of the Lyric Poet. In other words, although the tattletale buffer strata were "informing" Marse, actually hu (he or she) was in reality offering no real information. Trivia carried more notice than substance. Besides, trivia substituted for information was much more interesting because it made good storytelling. In common language, or in what proper people like to call vernacular language. On the plantation, they called it, "bull shitting, or, talking stuff."

The house Negroes spent much of their time bull shitting the master and his family by "talking stuff." And, it was funny to them. "They get a kick out of it." This subterfuge, i.e., talking stuff, permitted Lyric Poets as social commentators to spew anti-slavery commentary all over the place, and get away with it. Talking stuff simply meant the storyteller got away by making the story so real that the listener being entertained became so engrossed in the tale the she or he lost track of what was fact or fiction. How? The Master, as the most favored, is told,

"Dat nigga be singing dat Devil music and telling Hoo Doo stories, dems Devil Songs, "Marse" (master) you don't wanna hear dem Devil Songs, Marse Hunna.Naw! You don' wanna hear no Devil Songs," as she walks away grinning from ear to ear.

This off-handed offering of information had the effect of providing safety to the lyric poet: The term Devil music meant one thing to the least favored and a completely different thing to the most favored.The assumption of fornication being the only thing on the minds of the least favored gave the most favored a false sense of security.

Never did they think that the slave, occupier of the least favored position, would do such things as enlist in the U.S. military to the tune of 180,000 soldiers in the Army and be willing to lose over 30,000 to 40,000 in the War of Liberation, or be so crazy as to join that zealot John Brown to start the war for the liberation of the Least Favored people, the slave.

Never checking these outlawed stories out, the most favored were left to their own imagination to visualize how the least favored operated within the community thought to be beyond redemption: the most favored figured that this Devil Music was the cause of fornication and all other kinds of lewd sinful wicked ways that this music perpetuated among the slaves.

Little did the master know this lewd music was part of a repertoire that included a satire of the "marse's" (master's) family every night, never thinking that what the slaves were laughing over, way into the evening, were the tales about the "Bucksry," i.e., "the white man" that they never called "white"? We must recall that most of the tattle-tales were treated as "ole Annie," and "Uncle Ben" good Negress and "Boy" who knew their places within the culture of whiteness.

Getting word that someone from the Big House was coming, the lyric poet would segue into a blues tune about who's doing it to "whose ole' lady" or telling the story in song about "this is my man to night." These songs were humorous improvisations invented right there on the spot to give the impression that the performer was singing the same songs he or she was singing when the master appeared on the scene.

In turn, the most favored created their own fiction about how slaves operated. Cartoons, newsprint articles, wanted posters, and common gossip were the source of lies, distortions, and misinformation against the slave communities.

Bad Faith was the operational principle throughout this antebellum period. The effort at negation of the fallout that resulted from the physical violence permitted against the slave for "making the Overseer angry" was, in its crime, a successful time for the Lyric Poets.

The blues singers of Devil Songs, the only real processors and communicators of the culture of whiteness that practiced overt racism, were the most persistent social commentators by offering lyrics as a critique of the slave master. The Lyric Poet had the appropriately ideal milieu to create the forum worthy of these criticisms of the master class in song: Blues song.

Paying close attention to the historical development of Blues, it should be no surprise that this music reaches world acclaim. To survive, this creative art form —that was loosely structured music with a definitive lyric structure, where the lyricist would sing the first line twice with a minor change in the rendition the second time around— avoided the onslaught of the culture of whiteness.

Blues survived intact without the white middle class of the south participating in the process. Poor whites, however, did hear and begin to play what they heard coming from the Lyric Poets. The question is how could "Southern Culture" begin to evolve as a form while omitting its most creative contributors: the stolen people of Africa? How could that be?

To complete the story, as a continuation of bad faith, in spite of [the planter class'] efforts to hide these Devil Songs, designs were implemented to dispose of the Devil worship called "Hoo Doo" and its related forms, Devil songs and stories.

These forms were recognized as barriers to establishing a permanent institution of slavery. Fortunately they were not always successful in their efforts. Blues music, so called in the future, operated underground, oftentimes right in the midst of the Big House, with its true form reserved to be heard only by the faithful, i.e., those who really wanted to hear the old traditional music as it now sounded in the slaves' community.

Operating within a process of two opposing forces, my/this thesis says for there to be conflict, the least favored has to continue to practice the ways of life they are able to maintain, resistance or not, while the most favored continued to ban such artistic forms.

Moving the analysis forward, one form that came with the African survived despite constant bombardment. That form of distinction has been sustained intact: it is now referred to as Blues.

Despite the strength of the opposing forces, Blues continued to exist and persist according to its own principles of cultural formation juxtaposed with a practice that actively opposed the institution of slavery through criticisms offered as commentary in the form of song, oftentimes with the accompaniment of an instrument. Devil's music—as it was referred to by the most favored—as a form of social and political commentary became the mainstay of African existence.

What is important to recognize here is Blues retained the unique three minor tones throughout the entire history of this political struggle in the United States? Even when later generations would rename and rearrange its related musical forms to take the sting out of their sails, untouched Blues continue to serve as compilation of performance styles wedded to the community ways of New Africa.

Question

What is ugly language? When is it used? Who uses it most?

7. Politics and Aesthetics

Statement #6, Axiom 3

When a particular is considered the most favored, i.e., that particular is determined to occupy the most favored position of distinction, the name this particular assumes can be taken to indicate the value of the particular because of the position of distinction it occupies.

As politics and aesthetics inform each other they established as their interplay two processes: 1) the polity of culture established and sustained the conditions that allowed Blues forms to blossom; and 2) the musical form served as a continuum in the aesthetic appreciation of black music as attested to by the perception of its aficionados across the globe.

This process demonstrates how an instructor may apply an integrative approach to the research, teaching and the study of "aesthetics and culture." By creating a theme as a basis for the study of, e.g., Aesthetics and the Political Economy of Blues, as a primary form in the development of American culture, an instructor may teach a particular course in a holistic manner. Such a theme allows an instructor to include texts from music scores, film, sound tracks, economics, oral history, social history, cultural anthropology, African American literature, sociology, polity, geography, psychology and criticism, or any variation thereof, as source materials for the course. Having a working knowledge of all disciplines simultaneously allows an instructor to integrate or treat as interdisciplinary materials designed to enhance the course.

Question

What is the politics of aesthetics? Who tends to dominate? How? What does the form take? Offer examples!

8. Black Aesthetic

What is it?

Statement # 7, Axiom 4

When a name identifies each member as an equal within the form, any additional name assigned to that member indicates that within the form the additional name assigns a different value to that name.

A Black Aesthetic is the intuitive philosophical recognition of what constitutes a work of art (inclusive) as invented under/within the realm of Black Popular Culture. Black Popular Culture is a process of social intercourse that allows its audience to critique the value of the art as a subjectively arrived at process. That art, in this case music, is by performance standards an emotive intellectual intuitively pleasing piece. Be it a love song or social commentary, taste and preference are invented by creative labor. As a work process, a work in progress called creative labor invents the moment that its participants will witness the product in the making. Creative workers as laborers involved in the invention, serve as witnesses to and participants in the creative process as the work unfolds. This as a happening operates through its own dynamic.

What makes the dynamic creative and fascinating, thereby of aesthetic merit? The aesthetic merit is derived from neither the aficionados nor the group performing the music quite knowing where the performers are going with the particular creative work, a work that allows any number of improvisational possibilities that defy explanation. Very much aware of their roles as performers, their observations (listening) and informed discussions (playing) permit the invention of the work to unfold on stage as a performance demonstration. This mode of performance is arranged and conducted to allow the group performing that piece to express its full value. The level of creativity reached in their performance determines what makes that performance aesthetically pleasing as listened to by their aficionados. For the work to be judged of aesthetic merit that work or performance must be considered to fit within their definition of a black performance art.

The basic rule of a Blues-based performance art is the three (3) minor tones, the base of all black originated music; whatever genre derives from this music is influenced by or operates according to the rules governing the process of black music performance. That recognition constitutes agreement about what is creative yet utilitarian. The creative labor that produces these blues inventions is shared with and among that audience or, as Jim Hall, guitarist and composer said about Jazz as art music, "It does not play down to the audience." As its most common element, the audience may be present anywhere a performance is taking place. Moving to the present, performances now appear in places formerly considered "off limits," as well as the old venues always thought to be the appropriate location for "that type of music."

Blues Aesthetics, a Polity of Culture: a Position Theory applies the rules of Black Aesthetics to examine how Blues survived and evolved into the only original musical art in the uniquely American culture. The author has spent the last two decades researching and writing about the one musical form to survive as a continuum in a polity of culture whereby the terror of slavery, and sharecropping, were the norm of the day.

The continuum, Blues, transcended this terror as music in both time and location because, despite offerings to the contrary, Blues could not be an invention of the United States. There is no need for such a claim. There is no need because it came with the culture brought from Africa. Its archaic sound makes that case very evident. By the same token, Jazz as a creative black form, could not have been invented in any other place than United States and have retained the Blues element so apparent in Jazz's development and growth.

The invention of Jazz by African Americans in the United States was by no means an accident that could just as easily been invented by some other ethnic group, e.g., Italians. This is a preposterous notion that deserves no response. To call Jazz an "imperfect art with a questionable aesthetic" as Ted Gioia, a music critic, did in his work on Jazz, is only repeating James Harris, who said, `music [is] at best...an imperfect art.' Harris was an eighteenth century European philosopher that wrote three (3) volumes on music and the other arts as aesthetics.

All black music emanates from Blues and sounds the many different ways it does because it is an invention by the Least Favored of the United States. That statement should be a moot issue, but there is always the temptation to search for ways to deny its black beginnings. Blues is obviously older and different than anything the Africans came in contact with in this country.

Being older it is performed by norms other than those developed in Europe. In a kind of arrogance of authority, however, the claim was that Blues must conform to European standards of beauty or violate European tastes. Despite its violations of the old European norms of tastes, that is, what constitutes "beauty and the sacred," the artistic forms of Jazz established its own definition of beauty.

Blues evolved as a world-class integrative popular art form that applied lyrics and original musical scores improvised as a performance art. It has developed its own cultural form that informs the rest of society of what changes are at play. This communication is as easy as the three (3) traditional minor tones that inform the "world beat" heard throughout world popular culture today.

Question

What does the aesthetic process observe?

9. Black Popular Culture

What is it?

Statement #8, Axiom 2

To assign a particular process value greater than others, different names can be taken to indicate the value of each of the process assigned...To call a process by the name assigned indicates the value of the distinction assigned the process so named...Thus, to use that name to call this process again means the value is seen in the name called.

Black Popular Culture is a creative expression of the social intercourse that takes place as the Least Favored People, called the Black, struggle to create ways of defining themselves. It has a cultural dynamic that is always moving, flexible, fluid, and creatively changing. The culture of the slave as the Least Favored was reconstructed around a desire for freedom. Their aim was/is freedom, it was a preoccupation.

Despite the Most Favored people's occupation with a desire to create a totalitarian boundary around the Least Favored people, the Least Favored brought us music, dance, theatre, rhyme, verse, letters, song, worship, inventions, applied science, and other meaningful and aesthetically pleasing forms of expression.

As for the personalities who composed and orchestrated these new present cultural forms, it was an expression of an individual's conscious efforts to define one's self in a manner that struck a balance between self and community, i.e., a balance within the community in which one lived.

Question

What is Black Popular Culture" ?

10. Black Popular Culture

When did the aesthetic process begin?

Statement #9, Axiom 3

It is through the usage of symbols called words that we call the name of each boundary created to separate one form of distinction from another. It is through the usage of words that a language is developed to give name to the form of distinction.

Black Popular Culture (BPC) or Blues began as Africans struggled to retain, sustain and maintain those cultural forms that kept them in touch with the motherland upon arrival on the shores of the Americas. Retaining as many of her elements as possible did this. Retention came about through new symbol development. It was through symbols developed through the application of music and lyric that allowed Black Popular Culture to establish the base of its continuum.

By continuum here we mean a process is established that allows the culture to live and thrive as an entity unto itself while it informs the majority culture. These new symbol as expressed in music and language informed the development of "American" culture. Although the intent of the most favored was to redefine the entire tradition of the African Cultural Forms, thereby causing their entire negation as a people, the process of oppression that resulted was too imperfect to realize that goal.

The intent to offer only those elements that suited the most favored interest was implemented with uneven results and corresponding success. This made the process intended to redefine the least favored totally, that is, to make them into a new being, an unsuccessful effort. With this thought in mind we will put forth the following analysis.

This process of development of Black Popular Culture began during slavery. At that time, the critical mass of enslaved Africans in the slave society allowed them to congregate as a community and practice their cultural forms. These constituent residents resided in such numbers that they were de facto communities that amounted to hundreds of people who interacted daily.

It was within these communities that the music from Africa thrived. It was also revised and expanded, and exhibited a great deal of diversity. African hymns and secular music grew and expanded side by side until Christianity became a competing force with the traditional practices of worship and other forms of daily life.

As the slave—the least favored—practiced more aspects of the culture of whiteness more barriers were established to contradict practices thought to be in conflict with institutionalizing slavery. Religious practices

20

were the first to be outlawed. With converts to Christianity, traditional forms of praise were overturned and replaced. Hymns from Africa became new arrangements known as "spirituals". Undergoing many revisions, spirituals became acceptable because they spoke of those things thought complementary to the most favored.

The most favored obviously did not hear lyrics sung away from the "Big House." When heard by the Most Favored, these songs fell out of favor. Many became know as "secular" music. A genre of "secular" music that fell out of favor with the teachings of Christianity was indicated by the name "Devil's Music."

To the Most Favored all black music was "Devil's Music"; for the new converts to Christianity, the slave, these were "Devil Songs," called En-gung in Congo. The presenters of Devil Songs continued the tradition of offering social commentary about the local happenings of the day. I refer to these plantation community criers, who sang Devil Songs, as Lyric Poets. They are the primary creators of the black aesthetic or Black Aesthetics.

Question

When did Black Popular Culture Begin? Who are its authors?

11. Black Creative Music

"Aesthetics [and/or in] Politics"

What is the relationship?

Statement #10, Axiom 2

When the name of a cultural activity is indicated to express the value of that particular process the form of distinction is indicated by the name. In other words, the name is an indication of the degree of value derived by and/or assigned to that form of distinction. Put differently, a particular cultural activity thus indicated by an expression of the name is also an indication of the value assigned to that particular cultural activity as a form of distinction.

Black Popular Culture by its name +operates within a Polity of Culture. A Polity of Culture functions within the realm of politics and aesthetics. We might say politics meets aesthetics on the creative playground of Black Popular Culture. These complementarities serves to create such things as Black Music in its numerous genres. It is through the creation of Black Music the interplay between Aesthetics and Politics is acted out within this Polity of Culture.

Question

We might say politics meets aesthetics on the creative playground of Black Popular Culture. Explain. Two (2) pages

12. Black Creative Music

An Aesthetic Expression of BPC

What is it? (Secular)

Statement #11, Axiom 1

Once a distinction is made for each particular as separate activity, one activity cannot reach the other formation without crossing the boundary that makes the distinction.

Black music, as En-gung (Blues), is a musical form that came with the African from places like Congo/Angola, Mali, Senegambia, and other places from Angola across the continent to Ethiopia. Its origin is the peculiar three- (3) minor-tone sound that makes what we now call the "blue" note. It is this sound that serves as the grounding for all music secular and religious within the black idiom. It is referred to generically as Black Music, but commonly as Blues.

Aesthetically, Black Music's appeal to its listener is based on a sound that is often rhythmically enticing, e.g., Marvin Gaye's songs, with its strong sensual overtones is called Soul Music or Rhythm & Blues. Aficionados call it "getting in the groove." Thus, aesthetically speaking, Black Music violates the Kantian premise that implies music is 'purposive without purpose' because the purpose is to dance or to offer (entice) other means of self-expression.

Dance becomes a meditative experience that frees the spirit. Here the improvisational stream of this Black Creative Music may appear to offer the listener a tune that seems to present a "final without an end." The ongoing beat permits the dancer to reach cathartic levels of performance that often give the appearance of lewdness. However, there is no contradiction in the Black Creative Music and Black Dance because each derives it creativity from the three minor tones that govern the performance of Black Music as performed by that particular ensemble.Black Music has been in a struggle with the so-called mainstream, involving an effort to deny black music its rhythmic pulse and its free spirit to change. The most favored as Devil's Music identified this mode of performance. This all takes place while the music is receiving acceptance by the populace. To show acceptance, the populace names each new genre. All names defy the title Devil Music given to Black Music called Blues.

Problem

Black Music has been in a struggle with the so-called mainstream, involving an effort to deny black music its rhythmic pulse and its free spirit to change Explain what the struggle is? How is the struggle demonstrated? Give Example!

13. Black Creative Music, How is the Creativity Expressed?

Statement #12, Axiom 2

When a particular group activity is considered the Most Favored as a creative expression, i.e., the group that performs that activity occupies the Most Favored position of distinction among groups, the name the Most Favored group assumes, can be taken to indicate the value of the activity because of the position of distinction the group occupies.

The artistic beauty, brilliance, genius of creative labor, originality, and/or, inventiveness with purposeful expressions are the instances when aesthetics come alive in our examination of Black Music in general and Black Creative Music (Jazz) in particular. Blues through its most important forms will serve as the basis of this examination. Blues will serve as the means to discover how aesthetics evolve from an oppressed people's art within a polity of culture.

It is through its modern music, the offspring of Blues called Jazz or Improvisational Black Creative Music that we may follow the development of an aesthetic premise surrounding Black Creative Music. The assumption is that the position Black Creative Music has assumed as "world music" says there is an aesthetic governing its movement. Further, the premise is Black Creative Music did not assume this position without a struggle with the Most Favored of the first magnitude.

Question

How is the Creativity Expressed?

14. Black Creative Music

What is the particular? (Secular)

Statement #13, Basic Premise

We take as given the idea of distinction and the idea of indication7 and that in order to make an indication you must create a distinction. We take therefore the form of distinction for the form.

The particular is a struggle between the least favored who occupies the Black Position and the most favored who occupy the White position within a polity of culture. The actor is the Lyric Poet. The form of distinction that creates this dialectic involves Black Music in its struggle against the attempted dominance of the culture of whiteness.

During slavery this struggle was indicated by two genres: religious and secular.Here we deal with the secular realizing the there is no real distinction between the two when it comes to contemporary gospel. Further, there is no need to accept as given these pseudo distinctions because within "Improvisational" music all sense of genre is dismissed as nonexistent phantoms operating within the shallows of the dominant culture.

Question

What is the particular "Secular" song (inclusive) that Jazz Artists perform? What makes it particular? What is a particular? Give 5 examples using any form you can think of?

15. Black Creative Music

The Music of Improvisation

Statement #14, Axiom 2

When the name of a performance activity is indicated to express the creative value of the group that performs this activity the form of distinction is indicated by the name given, e.g., …In other words, the name is an indication of the degree of the value derived by and/or assigned to performance as a form of distinction.

Black Creative Music, often referred to as Jazz, is the music of improvisation and, often times, a creative melodic composition with a harmonic construct. One demonstrates one's creative nature by composing the music right there on the spot, "an original experience" according to Bobby Matherne, as the audience looks on in awe.

Creativity may be enhanced by actually writing a composition or creating a new arrangement of another song then improvising in solo form, or competitive poly forms, that embrace such combinations as duets and/or trios, as the musicians' interpretation of that piece. The idea is to perform the music at a level where the audience recognizes the creative talent through the inventiveness of the performer.

Many musicians do this by spontaneously making sounds that translate into colors harmonically arranged to create streams of thoughts expressed musically. These original thoughts an improvised composition at this level require great technical skills that come from constant practice and experimentation with scales, sound, texture, fluidity and other forms of musical distinction.

Constant practice is the manner in which one integrates the musical ideas into the conscious psyche of performance. Creativity is derived from this psyche. Such a psyche is able to act as producer of such thoughts that are expressed in the form of music. When performed in the manner intended, the audience and the performers immediately feel the aesthetic value of the performance simultaneously and in complementarities.

The usual requirements for a performer to become really gifted with his or her performance are those elements that are difficult to describe objectively. These elements are retained within the recesses of the other conscious. The other conscious is a gift of creativity and originality in that it elevates the performance to other levels.

Performance is everything in Black Creative Music. It is through one's performances that the aficionados become familiar with the works of a particular musician. We must recall here that the reason for this discussion is this creative invention referred to in the "vernacular" as Jazz was invented by the Least Favored people in society. As a matter of fact, all of Black Music came from The Least Favored people who are called black.

Thusly stated, "Black" is both a color and a position. Aesthetically speaking, as a color, it is the least liked, except in automobiles, dresses, suits, shoes and women's under- garments. As a social position, black is the Least Favored in any society that operates within a classification system, what others prefer to call a "class arrangement." Thus to have a music aesthetic developed by and from the works of the Least Favored people as an original cultural form in that society is a sufficient rationale for the Most Favored not to offer accolades to the Least Favored musicians.

To advance that musical form to the level of high performance, whereby the actual gift of the presenter is omnipresent within that performance deserves recognition of high merit. Yet within the society in which this Improvisational music was invented a denial of its existence and non-recognition of its performers as artists of the first order is still a problematic that has to be addressed.

A type of music that it is clearly an art form that serves as the base of American music should receive accolades in the form of state support as do the European classical forms and the teaching of the Humanities, Sciences, Management and other social forms considered important to the operation of social intercourse.

As it is, this is the contradiction faced by performers of the music who come from the Least Favored cultural form in the United States. It has often been difficult to overcome. Facing this contradiction as an American and black, in an open society that promotes white as the Most Favored color, the treatment can be difficult to phantom.

The notion of applying "color" literally to people's skin tone should seem too ludicrous to be taken seriously. However, such arbitrary definitions can exist when distinctions are made between people as indicated by "skin color." Skin color becomes a position. Positions are classified as unequal, according to the mark of distinction as indicated by the name and position that is assigned to that color.

To add insult to injury, the makers of the cultural forms that are adopted in this society are literally made invisible in an attempt to marginalize their existence. To ignore one's birth parents in an effort to have them disappear is tantamount to destroying them through denial that operates as a form of non-recognition. "Nigger as far as I am concerned you do not exist in my mind. I do not see you, hear you, or in any way acknowledge your existence. So get over it. It is not my problem."

The point is, despite all that I have said regarding Black Creative Music, with a few exceptions, it is not supported with subsidy. On the other hand, in New York City music that has it origin in Europe receives millions of dollars in funds from federal, state, city, and private donations.

If Black Creative Music were not of equal quality to other art forms as a performance and concert art that receive subsidy from the state and private donations, maybe an argument could be made for not offering public support for the music. However, the music is recognized as exhibiting its own unique quality as an art form of a creative nature. The polity of culture serves as the mechanism for awarding merit to those considered as having made significant contributions to the advancement of the arts to popular culture.

Some maintain that to subsidize art will make the potential artists lazy and mediocre. It's interesting that when it comes to science or technological advancements no arguments are raised within the United States about gifts to research universities, institutes, and the like.

There is an obvious double standard used within the polity of culture that maintains that when a product emanates from the Least Favored, it deserves little or no support except that offered by the marketplace of listeners who prefer that particular style of music. What we find is, despite the neglect of Black Creative Music from its base, Blues, to most of its listeners, 'Jazz' music continues to evolve new genres in a very frequent and creative manner. Just when one thinks there can be no more, another genre arises as if from ashes of the Phoenix.

How is this possible when no other musical form the world over seems to be able to do this? It is the three minor tones that permit this advancement in Black Music. It is the milieu of the creators that establishes the pre-conditions and maintains the conditions that encourage Black Music creativity. Black Creative Music is where the most advancement has been made in terms of music transition and transformation.

As it changes each new genre continues to be judged on the merit of performance. Aesthetically speaking Blues as a continuum continues to offer world culture a musical form that is unique, challenging, beautiful and intellectually stimulating with an offering of "good taste" to its aficionados.

Good taste implies a sense of feeling good about what one just heard presented by the musicians in their performance. Simply put, Blues aesthetic is a subjective approach to appreciation. Aesthetically speaking, one can only appreciate what one feels about the music. Without feeling Black Creative Music is tasteless.

This means it is without substance, a creative product that can only be realized through the creative labor of the performing musicians. Thus when it is said, "there was no feeling in the music tonight," the implications are that the performers are unable to reach the essence of Black Creative Music because they show no emotive qualities in their characterization of the process. There is no expression because it is lost in lack of feeling in the characterization of the piece. This loss of feeling offers no emotive substance that allows aficionados to feel the presence of the night's performance. Thus, for the aficionados that performance left no aesthetic appeal although the music may have been well presented, i.e., with the proper technique and knowledge of the music.

Back to the existential question, does Black Creative Music have a governing aesthetic? Yes, it does, unequivocally. What is it? It is the same process that governs all aesthetically pleasing music. Then, what is the problematic? The most favored want to take the birth- right from the least favored: it means control the masters. The most favored derive the primary benefits while the musicians get what remains, if there are any remains. In essence, if the most favored cannot control the means of production, they want to control its distribution.

Control over the distribution allows the Most Favored to censor what lyrics are not allowed. So, although the war to destroy Black Popular Culture was not won by the most favored, their ability to market distribution gave them control over who and when the music was to be played until the new technology gave the consumer the appearance of the ability to play that role.

A serious disadvantage was realized by the makers of Black Music when they were juxtaposed with record producers whose venture capital allowed them to record the "master" of a small unknown musician, pay them a small fee, e.g., $200, to sign the contract, and keep the master as their own copyright.

The control of the musician's master gives the producer total control over the outcome of any recording made by music maker. The failure to be able to defend the record producer forces Black Creative Musicians to depend more on live performance for their work to be heard and seen. However, it is these live concerts that often produce the best music from most of these performances. It is here that the aficionados are allowed test their aesthetic judgment about what is good and what is bad on a given day.

Question

Explain what improvisations are. How does one do it? One paragraph. One sentence. One page.

16. The Culture Industry

A Post Marxist Point of Departure

A Point of Departure

Statement # 15, Axiom 1

Once a distinction is made for each formation, groups on each side of the boundary, being distinct can be identified as different. There can be no distinction of groups without motive. There can be no motive unless these groups are thought to differ in value. The group that holds the Most Favored form of distinction is considered to hold the most value. The intent and/or desire of the Least Favored group are to cross the boundary into the position occupied by that group. The value assumed by the group wanting to cross indicates the greater value awarded to and assumed by the Most Favored group.

Although, Theodor Adorno was at Columbia University, right in the heart of Harlem, at the time when Be Bop was at its height, he never would have understood BPC in general and Be Bop in particular. However that is no reason to dismiss his concept of the culture industry. I therefore take the name as a point of departure. This brief analysis of the culture industry will focus on the Political Economy of Black Music rather than a critique of his thesis, which others have done quite meticulously.

The culture industry, according to the Theodor Adorno theory, is a process whereby art – in this case music – is made into a commercial industry that codifies music into a product that can be bought and sold within the market place. The process that unfolds is the commoditization of the Least Favored.

Those co modified through creative labors assume the status of producers as a factory worker does an automobile or a bar of soap. It is now a commodity no more, no less, to be bought and sold to consumers whose tastes are thought to be individually arrived upon. The Least Favored must serve as the distributor and consumer simultaneously.

It is now a commodity no more, no less. As such, one can go into a virtual store download the music onto a disc or MP3, iPod, iTunes or whatever the latest model of down loading is and purchase the product sight unseen. In this case, one does have the opportunity to hear the music one is downloading and purchase it simultaneously. This means popular music now sells at a pace that defies thought.

According to Adorno, it is the process of codification that allows one to distinguish "high art," in this case, Jazz, from "low art," Rhythm/rock and roll/Blues, or in the case of "high art," "classical" from "pop" music. It is here where the contradiction arises. Purely speaking, Jazz, i.e., Black Creative Music, requires the same level of musical training as classical music.

However, the substance Jazz is arbitrarily declared a "pop art" form. It is supposed that there is no basis in substance for this difference in classification. Such thinking places Jazz, a Black Art, in a situation that as an art form, its worth is never recognized for its true value to the culture industry. Put more in terms of how it is intended, "What rhyme or reason would anyone want to claim that Jazz is not a "pop" art?"

This is clearly a misnomer. Therefore, the false labeling or classification is subjective and without foundation. This falsity is a bias that places a great burden on aficionados of Jazz because with such a listing this artistic music receives neither the support from the Most Favored as high art – except unevenly in some locations- nor the promotion to sell as a pop art within the market place of popular culture.

The false listing places Jazz within a neuter territory as an art form. Jazz, in effect, suffers a non-recognition status in that it is neither pop (rock) nor classical (European). The denial of Jazz as an equal to European art music in effect is an attempted negation of America's unwanted child.

Despite this status, as a negation of the negation, Jazz continues to attract the most gifted and creative musicians to its performance stage while it continues to serve as the vanguard of a classic musical form yet produced by musicians any place else in the world.

Unlike the old classical music of Europe and Asia, it has not become fossilized as one might think of classical music. Plus, all of its respective genres remain alive and active as performance music. However, unlike rock music, it does not receive the gigantic promotions, distributions, and sales in the market place of commercial music; nor does it receive the state and private donations from the upper middle class, the American equivalent to the European bourgeoisie.

As a "pop art" it does not receive the promotion, distribution and other means of financial support that is awarded pop musicians whom the record industry wants to promote and support in the market place. The rationale for this lack of support is that Black Creative Music does not bring in the billions of dollars that one can expect from popular music. The same analysis applies to "classical" music. Yet, it is thought to be uncouth for a city of any worth within the United States not to have a symphony orchestra that is supported by a collection of finances from the State and/or private donations.

There is a kind of oddity here. There is some a level of financial support for Jazz concerts in places like New York City when a member of the Most Favored feels that there should be some financing for free concerts for public audiences.

However, this support is very limited and not necessarily consistent. Financial support does not translate into the financial rewards approaching the magnitude of that brought in by the classical or pop music. Again, when a member of the Most Favored decides to support Jazz, those musicians tend to command more money per performance than comparable or even better artists performing at an event that are sponsored by members of the Least Favored position.

Even when it is acknowledged that the event sponsored by the Least Favored was better attended and the performance was more exciting than one sponsored by members of the Most Favored Position, there is little or no State funding offered to these sponsors. The position of the Most Favored offers them an advantage never realized by those less favored.

It is this process that makes Black art music into an underdeveloped and poorly recognized commercial industry of culture. It is supposed that this is how music as an industry participates in the commercialization of art as a product to be bought and sold on the open market. The rationale of such treatment is this culture industry is expected to respond according to the laws of supply and demand.

No high art responds to the laws of supply and demand except on the low end of commercial demand. However, there may be some individual artists who may on occasion have luck in the market place at a given time. It appears to be more luck than any real genius that is rewarded. This means that because of its nature and the real contribution Black Creative Music makes to those other music genres that are able to function in the market place, Jazz should be rewarded accordingly.

On what basis does Jazz deserve more financial support and social recognition? On the basis that the contributions it makes to the development of new musical forms, ideas and innovative concepts that result from the experimentation that goes on in Jazz makes it qualify for greater support than is given to date.

The new sound equations that pop music benefits from should suggest to a learned society that with more support the society is better off aesthetically and culturally. These new sounds in turn are what allow pop artists to simplify what they hear into a marketable product the public can relate to.

This in turn allows pop "artists" to reap financial riches in the market place. This same analysis applies to Blues. Blues acts as the base and originator of new forms of sound that causes other genres to hear things that may be applied to their music that becomes a hit.

It may be the same song but done by a member of the Most Favored in a more assessable sound that allow the song to become a hit. If the Blues composer (inclusive) does not protect him or her self, that person may lose all rights to the material composed and sung prior to a record company finding someone else to record the tune for public consumption. On the other hand, a record company may reap millions or even billions of dollars off of one Jazz masterpiece, i.e., Kind of Blue by Miles Davis.

The down side is what amounts to plagiarism is encouraged and permitted on the part of the Most Favored. What makes this plagiarism so disheartening to the Least Favored people in the Americas in general and the United States in particular is how plagiarism promotes having the music's originality attributed to those who have no foundation to create the musical forms they take.

What is further disheartening is how the music owners of the recording industry will tell an artist what he or she must call his or her genre. The best examples of this are Elvis Presley and Jimmie Hendricks. Both wanted to be thought of as Blues singers and musicians. However, the A&R producers insisted on listing both as Rock 'n Roll performers. Here the Law of Position is best applied because color is not the issue. Elvis was called "white" while Hendricks was called "Black".

Yet, each was, at different times, forced to embrace a name neither felt expressed who they were and what type of music they performed. Each was placed in this position because both came from the Least Favored people in the American cultural forms. Presley came from "po' white trash" while Hendricks was of mixed Native and African American origins.

Thus regardless of national classification each came from the Least Favored position in the United States, and both were treated accordingly: Neither had much to say over their future. Both died tragic deaths that made them immortals and their recordings classic fixtures that will keep their record companies receiving royalties into infinity.

31

Although Blues, called En-gung by the Mbuwun people of the Bndundu Province, Congo, is the only original art form to evolve within the confines of these United States, it is still classified as "low art" or, when one is being polite, "folk" art.By placing Blues in a category that never permits it to gain an advantage, even members from the most favored seldom receive the rewards one receives from performing pop music.

The fact is Blues should never be placed out side of the forum of art that permits it to benefit from the musical force it offers to world culture. As the producer of world music, it suffers from a similar position of a cotton picker who produces the cotton, yet can show little reward for that production.

The bias perpetuated against the least favored in this society, permits the culture industry to realize massive gains without investing in the product it receives from that position. What we are saying here is the culture industry tends to reflect the biases inherent in the overall society. One would think that with a producer deriving a living from a performance art for public consumption, the consumers who benefit from this product would provide a means of equalizing the gains awarded to the producer. That said the culture industry changes nothing.

Question

What is the culture industry? Who are its participants? What things do they do? Who is the author of the Culture Industry? What did that person write?

17. Me Thinks

Statement # 16, Axiom 2

It is through the usage of symbols called words that we establish language as a means of indication of the motive that brings about a form of distinction. It is through the usage of language that we establish how crossing a boundary of distinction is determined or when (how, where) that crossing is permitted. It is the usage of language that the motive has as a basis of expression for a form of distinction that is made.

The word Jazz is a very aesthetically pleasing name. If the basis of its claim is in, "I want to make love to you baby." I think that the word tells the story of what the creative energy is in this music called Jazz. Jazz in its most pleasing quality reveals how easily one can move from a melodic sound that is presented in harmony, to a harmonic blend of voicing that makes the melody a collective sound. Jazz voicing makes the music sensually pleasing when it is presented in an orchestration.

Supposedly, Jazz had its origin in original sin: "lewd fornication in the den of inequity, the Devil's Church, the place of sinful luster." As a complement to this least favored's space, the location of the beginning Jazz, the term, beatifies the position of love making as a continuum that never ends.

One loses contact with the actual space-time when the music is at its finest. Jazz, whether referred to as African American, Classical or Black Creative, or Improvisational Music, is still a sensual construct of sound that relieves the tension of everyday experiences.

Bluntly stated, Jass is a name we do not need to be ashamed of because of its origin. Although, "I wanna jass (sex) you up" may have been sung with a lewd intent and with ill begotten thoughts, the thoughts were not ill-conceived feelings of rudeness. Thus, to call this creative music Jazz, i.e., after the lewd lyrics of some Lyric Poet called a Blues musician, who was black (in position occupied), do really these same people invent a complement to the music?

Singing the song with the chorus mentioned above gave name to a new process. The new process was symbolized by one letter representing an elbow (J) design of a saxophone, the other (A) with legs bent and spread apart, ending with two letters (SS) with the shape of two snakes makes Jass the music of original improvisation, an aesthetic of Black Art.

So the Lyric Poet called it what it was, Jass. The word made sense. However, it was through the creative innovation of other musicians that the word Jass became known as Jazz, thus giving it a different aesthetic ring with more flavors. This was Black Music in its most risqué form and delivery. Only the low life or simple people were responsible for risqué displays.

33

These people were from the Least Favored Position in society.After all, all of Black Music comes from the Least Favored people. The name, Jazz, as a gift to a musical form was not intentional I assure you, but it applied to and was immediately accepted by the Least Favored as their name for this good music presented in a manner they had never heard before.

Put differently, it is the name of the Least Favored who has created all of the new music that permeates world culture, let us allow their voices to be heard using a name they created and love to use so dearly.

Jazz (Black Creative Music) is really the product of Blues aesthetics operating within a polity of culture. Now it is recognized as the contributor to, as inventors of, world popular culture. Being so, that recognition appears more acceptable if the honorees are descendants of people from the most favored position.

Their contributions are offered as more accepting from a member of the Most Favored. When their cultural icons embrace this vernacular form of music called Jazz, the least favored music is now legitimate within their boundary of civilization as defined by the culture of whiteness.

With Black Creative Music emanating from the least favored position, i.e., Black people, there is an attempt of the most favored to apply the rules differently when it comes to recognizing the Black Arts. In the United States, the Black Arts are judged as not holding to same significance to world culture as any art form that has as its base the culture of whiteness.

That judgment operates without merit because as far as world popular culture is concerned, the proof is in the putting.Black Music in general and Black Creative Music in particular are equal to all and second to none. It is currently the most popular musical form in world culture.

The assumption of the dominant culture is because the birth place of Black Creative Music, is suppose to be the rural South, it can never expect to receive the same statute as that of "classical" music brought from Europe to the United States, by the Most Favored.

This assumption allows two processes to evolve for the Most Favored: taking control of the intellectual property from the Least Favored, as their own without proper compensation, then selling the products derived from this false property ownership in the market place, thus gaining the material and financial benefits from such "ownership" at the total expense of the Least Favored, the creators of the product.

By maintaining such "ownership," the propaganda of the Most Favored can sustain a constant perception of Black Creative Music is of less value because it comes from the least favored position. The Least Favored Position negates any idea that Black Creative Music or the Black Arts in general can ever offer any value comparable to that retained for music identified as coming from the most favored position.

Despite the omnipresent effort to belittle cultural forms from the least favored position, without subsidy Black Creative Music has attracted the most gifted musicians from across the globe to its performance stages. The attraction is its openness to innovation, change and other elements of creative energy that defy definition.

The intent of this discourse is to create conversation around a different way of looking at aesthetics and politics, aesthetics in politics, politics in aesthetics and political aesthetics. Within the discourse we employ A Position Theory as a mode and means of examination.

By offering A Position Theory as a mode and means to examine social intercourse aesthetics is offered as a form of distinction that is indicated by the name Blues Aesthetics. Blues Aesthetics operates within a polity of culture.

Operating within the context of Black Creative Music, i.e., the Black Arts, Blues has evolved its own aesthetic principles of continuum. Within the continuum of Blues other Black Music development introduced a code of conduct regarding performance that evolved into a process that is infinite musically and lyrically.

The code is expansive in that it allows levels of high performance for musicians so willing. Where no barriers beyond ones ability, perseverance, determination, and genius exist, gifted talent from the Least Favored Position find Blues forms willing configurations to compose within for any one so musically inclined.

The problematic is one must be willing to suffer the potential set backs that are always or at least oftentimes apparent for the people of the Least Favored Position who serve as the base of society. That position at the base allows others in more favored positions to misname, and therefore misrepresent, the base by offering it the name "bottom." "The bottom" is the lowest social ranking one can attain within the human intercourse called society.

However, to use the term as in the "Black Bottom Café" gives flavor to that name. To use Black Bottom, which is considered a racist/sexist representation of a Black Woman's behind, as the name of a Jazz Nite Spot, means that Jazz is played there. Does that not keep the stereotype about Black people alive? People at the bottom occupy the black position.

Jazz is performed in a nightclub with a lewd name for a Black Woman that complements the type of music one should expect to hear by going there. Is that a negation of the negation? Or, is it an extension of the negation?

In the United States the position black represents every "color' "race" "ethnic group" including religious practices that occupy the Least Favored people in this society. However, the group that owns the official definition of the position called Black is people who claim African ancestry. Their "color", meaning skin tone, makes them simultaneously black in color and position.

The position has its basis in the legal institution of slavery. American slaves were the "have-nots" or the untouchables, called the black, within this social context. Using the term "the Bottom" to advertise that this place is a Jazz Club seems to give the music that part of the aesthetic that creates the mystique so much apart of Jazz today, part fiction, part myth and part fact. Do we want to keep that alive as part of the Black Aesthetic?

It was the black that created the original music of the New World Colony called the United States. The music, Black Creative Music, often referred to as Jazz, offers an aesthetic system that has quickly become the artistic mode for creative musicians interested in expansive and experimental forms.

Blues form is the most expansive music discovered to date. The three minor tones permit any equation to formulate within the genius of the music maker. With that knowledge it is no accident that these three tones serve as the root music for blues, spirituals, gospel, jazz, ragtime, stride, boogie woogie, swing, bebop, Afro-Cuban Jazz, cool, rhythm/rock 'n roll/blues, soul, disco, reggae, Afro Pop, and hip hop. Avant-garde, free form, experimental, ragtime and third stream integrated African-European musical forms into a performance mode uniquely black.

The ability to adapt to the culture of whiteness without ever loosing its essence is what made Blues Black Music. Blues simultaneously has become the original and only American form of music performed to survive in to-to by African people in the United States.

This music was performed during the growth and development of American Civilization. It was the country background in places like Alabama, Arkansas, Georgia, Louisiana, Mississippi, the Carolinas,

Tennessee and Texas that permitted Blues to survive in tact through compositions by unknown Lyric Poets and the likes of a Paul Laurence Dunbar, Bessie Smith, Memphis Minnie, Ma' Rainey, Sterling Brown and Langston Hughes.

Style and Aesthetics

Jazz is a form that allows the performer to apply the techniques of improvisation. Improvisation by its nature is an original happening that may appear as a spontaneously arrived at presentation. It does this by offering a performance governed by the blues aesthetic rules of style. Style is a mode of expression that allows a musician or musicians to distinguish themselves as performers of art music. Styles allow musicians to establish their unique ways of playing or vocalizing their presentations as an art form done as performance. Style permits a musician to "say what he or she says as creatively as the moment allows."Style is how the musician's ideas form a sound that an aficionado judges to be presented in a manner, which is unique.In short, style as a way of presenting music artistically. The aesthetic appreciation results when the uniqueness of the performance offers the audience a feeling of being there when it all happened.

What is a mark of distinction? How does one create/establish a mark of distinction? Do word symbols play a role in creating/establishing another's mark of distinction? Give examples.

18. After Thought

The Applause

Statement #17, Axiom 3

When the name of the group is indicated to express the value of the group the form of distinction is indicated by the name. In other words, the name is an indication of the degree of value derived by and/or assigned to that form of distinction.

Nothing is more revealing about a musician's performance than when one hears the name called is complemented with a loud applause followed by a standing ovation right after that's musician's ensemble has just completed a magnificent performance. The applause makes the performer feel ecstatic with delight. Nothing can be of more worth than the feel of recognition. This acknowledgement encourages the performer to compose more original works that appear to be pleasing to the audience's ear.

So the question remains,

WHY HAVE JAZZ MUSICIANS BEEN ASSIGNED THE LEAST FAVORED POSITION WITHIN THE CULTURE INDUSTRY? WHY HAVE THE MUSICIANS WHO HAVE CREATED AND CONTINUE TO CREATE AN ORIGINAL MUSICAL FORM NOT RECEIVED THE RETURNS COMMENSURATE WITH THEIR CONTRIBUTION TO INTELLECTUAL AND SOCIAL INTERCOURSE? WHY HAVE THE CREATIVE LABORERS WHO ARE THE INVENTORS OF DIVERSITY NOT BEEN OFFERED THE ACCLAIM USUALLY AWARDED TO SUCH ADVANCEMENTS?

APPENDIX

Historical Interplay between Specialization and Integration

Ever since the appearance of the social sciences as separate domains of inquiry in the late nineteenth century, an interplay has occurred between movements for greater specialization on the one hand and efforts at interdisciplinary integration on the other hand.1

Auguste Comte, one of the founders of modern social science, envisaged a unified social science. In the middle of last century he expressed a concern that specialization in human thought, while permitting a "felicitous development of the spirit of detail otherwise impossible . . . spontaneously tends . . . to snuff out the spirit of togetherness, or at least to undermine it profoundly."2

Toward the end of the nineteenth century, the American Social Science Association was struggling heroically to keep the social sciences together and focused on solving human problems. But the centrifugal forces of specialization and professionalization associated with the industrialization of America spurred the establishment of one separate social science discipline after another. With the founding of the American Political Science Association in 1903 and the American Sociological Society in 1905 the original Social Science Association was reduced to an empty shell that totally collapsed a few years later.3 Yet, ironically, Professor Albion Small, one of the founders of the American Sociological Society and the first editor of its journal, wrote in 1910:

Specialized science, whether physical or social, inevitably passes into a stage of uncorrelated scientific piece-work. In this stage of dismemberment, science is as inconclusive through its lack of coherence as it was in an earlier period from its superficiality. That is, it then had breadth without depth, it now has depth without breadth.4

The Social Science Research Council was organized in the 1920's with the explicit purpose of providing a forum for integration across disciplines.5 And in the 1930's, Otto Neurath at the University of Chicago initiated an impressive effort to prepare an *International Encyclopedia of Unified Science.*

Despite these efforts, a painful fact of reality was stated by R. S. Lynd in 1939:

The failure of the social sciences to think through and to integrate their several responsibilities for the common problem of relating the analysis of parts to the analysis of the whole constitutes one of the major lags crippling their utility as human tools of knowledge.6

The problem and the need have not disappeared to this day. In fact, the situation may have worsened in some respects while improving in others. Disciplines and sub-disciplines are now more numerous and more firmly entrenched in the academy than ever. Yet the social movements of the sixties spawned several new inter-disciplines which are still in existence. Moreover, the prevalent Vocationalism of the seventies has shifted attention from the theoretical to the seventies has shifted attention from the theoretical to the applied fields of study, which are by necessity interdisciplinary in nature3

An interdisciplinary program that offers a curriculum explicitly designed to help students overcome some of the fragmentation of knowledge soon discovers that neither students nor faculty are satisfied with a program that does not go beyond strident critique of excessive specialization or exhortations to "put things together, to make man whole again," no matter how cathartic this may be. To further complicate matters, the label "interdisciplinary" itself became a buzzword for all the curricular reforms introduced in the late sixties and intended to make college education "more relevant." A plethora of "innovative" "interdisciplinary" programs sprouted up all over the country. Many of these were stronger on admirable sentiment than on intellectually defensible content or structure.

Interdisciplinary faculty had to articulate more effectively just what it was they were about so that they could answer the students who wanted to know what interdisciplinary studies were as well as to respond to skeptical colleagues in the traditional departments who were displaying an increasingly jaundiced eye towards "all this interdisciplinary stuff."

During the turmoil of the late sixties I wrote a small paper in which I attempted to make some basic distinctions between various kinds of interdisciplinary approaches in the social sciences.7 A few years later the seminal OECD study appeared, entitled *Interdisciplinarity: Problems of Teaching and Research in Universities*. Not only did this study set the framework for almost all subsequent discussion on the subject, but it also established the term "interdisciplinarity" in our professional jargon.8

The early 1970's also witnessed that diffusionary phenomenon of an idea spreading like wildfire through the nation's higher academies, namely Thomas Kuhn's *Structure of Scientific Revolutions*.9 All at once, anyone not talking about the "paradigms" of scientific disciplines was hopelessly out of it. That included social scientists, even though Kuhn himself had called their disciplines "pre-paradigmatic." Interestingly, Kuhn's book is part of the first and only published volumes of Professor Neurath's *International Encyclopedia of Unified Science* mentioned above. Kuhn's work in the history of science does help us to clarify the meaning of that fundamental concept, academic discipline.4

II. The Concept of Discipline

The term discipline refers to areas historically delineated by departmentalization. Thus in the social sciences the generally recognized disciplines are anthropology, economics, history, geography, political science, psychology and sociology. Within each discipline there are rational, accidental and arbitrary factors responsible for the peculiar combination of subject matter, techniques of investigation, orienting thought models, principles of analysis, methods of explanation and aesthetic standards. Each social science discipline looks at a part of the world of human behavior in its own peculiar way.10 They have divided this same material field into "several conceptually distinct levels, aspects, functions and dimensions."11

In fact, disciplines in any field are characterized by their special filtering and interpreting devices. Over time, the members of a particular discipline acquire a shared set of principles by which their inquiries are directed. These principles direct the disciplinarian to observe certain facts out of the virtually infinite variety of possibilities. These facts are organized by the conceptions -- the "make sense patterns" -- of the discipline, and thus are given meaning. As Joseph Schwab has so persuasively demonstrated, The scientific knowledge of any given time rests not on the facts but on selected facts and the selection rests on the conceptual principles of the inquiry. Moreover . . . it is of the facts interpreted, and this, too, depends on the conceptual principles of the inquiry.12

The structure of the discipline, therefore, tends to determine what aspect of reality is studied, how it is understood, and the relative validity of the descriptive and explanatory statements derived therefrom.13

Kuhn's discussion of paradigms makes essentially the same argument about what guides scientific inquiry; only the concept paradigm is used to stand for all the elements defining a discipline mentioned above. In his 1969 postscript, Kuhn labeled the "common possession of the practitioners of a particular discipline" its "disciplinary matrix" and discussed four components: symbolic generalizations, beliefs (including beliefs in particular models), values and exemplars (the previously successful problem-solving approaches). He now wishes to limit the meaning of paradigm to the last component, but admits that it will be difficult, as it has "assumed a life of its own."14

Whatever one calls the basic shared views of a group of scholars-teachers-researchers organized into a discipline, there is no doubt about their existence or their impact on the transmission and pursuit of knowledge. Speaking of higher education, Joseph Kockelmans recently observed, Our world has become splintered and fragmented by the fact that each individual discipline has developed its own general conceptual framework, its own set of theories and methods, all of which in the final analysis rest on implicit philosophical assumptions and ultimately lead to different conceptions of the world.15

In other words, each disciplinary community shares its own unique world view.16

Robert Redfield described world-view as the way a group of people organize their conceptions, their feelings about their experience and things in that experience. It is a "stage set." "World views are visions outward from the self . . . and conceptions of everything." They contain a sense of order, of what is real and how knowledge is obtained. They are the "underlying premises" of thought.17

The advantages of using "world view" as a conception in understanding disciplines are several. Worldview is a universal concept. Every culture, every subculture and every group has one. Students can more easily acquire an understanding of something if they themselves have experienced it. No arguments arise over whether a group has acquired one yet or not. The degree of unanimity surrounding a group's world-view is a question to explore, but not its presence or absence. Furthermore, world-view points to the conceptual construction, which is used by a group to interpret reality. In my view, it is that conceptual framework, the associated images and metaphors, plus the understandings of relationships among them which pre-eminently influence how the members of one discipline think in contrast to the members of another discipline. It is not subject matter or the naming of a single central concept that identifies the essence of a discipline, but the predominant thought model or models. "Any kind of discourse in the social sciences presupposes a model which specifies the basic relationships of human beings to the environment. This is true even when the details of the model are not spelled out."18

Economics, which probably has the most conceptual order among the social sciences, has its market model. It is a fully articulated logical model with assumptions on human nature; a specified set of roles and relationships; a single, commensurable, all-pervasive indicator; a calculus; a mode of representation and a predictable set of consequences if certain conditions hold. Does it not meet Heckhausen's "most crucial criterion level of a discipline -- the level of theoretical integration"?

Each empirical discipline tries to reconstruct the 'reality' of its subject matter in theoretical terms in order to get hold of that overwhelmingly complex reality, in order to understand, explain and predict phenomena and events involving the subject matter.19

5

Certainly the degree and type of theoretical integration varies from one discipline to another, due largely to accidents of historical configurations. The range in political science from philosophers to behaviorists produces compartmentalized subfields; yet the elan of identity with the overall discipline manages to hold the parts together. In other disciplines, such as psychology, different schools of thought compete to explain the same subject matter: behaviorists vs. psychoanalysts vs. phenomenologist's etcetera. As Professor Newell contends, these competing schools of thought do complicate matters further.20Nevertheless; there are underlying premises which members of disciplinary groups do share and which distinguish one group from another. Would anyone deny the existence of important world-view differences between political scientists and psychologists? The problem comes in identifying them, describing them and finding ways to verify them.

Another advantage of using world-view as the primary means of distinguishing one discipline from another is its efficiency. No one can learn all the research specialties, techniques and findings of a single discipline, let alone several. Nor can very many individuals be expected to achieve enough conditioning in several disciplines so that they fully internalize their respective paradigms. Needed is a consciously explicit, feasible and valid device for acquiring an effective comprehension of the key distinguishing attributes of the social science disciplines. World view meets that need.Finally, worldview provides a conceptual handle for making distinctions between different interdisciplinary approaches. To what degree components are coordinated and conceptually ordered provides one axis of differentiation. Shared underlying premises serve as another basis for categorizing.

Reference

Miller, .Raymond C. 1981. VARIETIES OF INTERDISCIPLINARY APPROACHES IN THE SOCIAL SCIENCES: A OVERVIEW Professor of Social Science San Francisco State University Presented

42

at the Third Annual Conference of The Association for Integrative Studies April 3, 1981 Published in Issues in Integrative Studies: An Occasional Publication of the Association for Integrative Studies (1982) pp. 1-37 Copyright 1981 Raymond C. Miller.

COMPLEMENTARITIES

THRU

Dialogues, Plays & Critiques

Part 2.

Read Aloud

BLACK CREATIVE MUSIC

[Jazz]
Delridge La Veon Hunter

a poem
spiritual nourishment
jazzed up
improvised
like a spontaneous composition
searching for
searing towards
a new way

Characters

Don Quinn

Edward

A definition.

A spiritual nourishment by a `jazzed up' improvisation, i.e., a spontaneous composition, searching for, searing toward something new, different, yet, always of the same.

The dialogue.

{A recording can be heard in the background:Charles Mingus, bass, bandleader; Ted Curson, trumpet; Eric Dolphy, reeds; Booker Ervin, tenor saxophone; Dannie Richmond, drums; Bud Powell, piano; at Antibes.)

Don Quinn

`When you talk about the jazz worker, you have to admit that the blues musician is the lowest member on the totem pole.Blues musicians occupy the lowest position of the least favored.'

Edward

`Economically speaking!?'

Don Quinn

`Of course!Socially, the blues musician is held in high esteem in some circles, depending on who it is. But none of the musicians who play that music makes very much money.'

Edward

`So so, but that's true by and large.Especially if you are referring to jazz or what I call creative musicians. They are truly the jazz workers.Seldom can they work at their profession without finding other means of employment at different intervals in their lives.Many simply become full time employees in other professions, especially, when they relate to jazz or music.'

Don Quinn

`At some point in their lives.'

Edward

`At some point in their lives! But today we see it more so than ever.You can't be in a band full-time.'

Don Quinn

`There are exceptions.'

Edward

`Not and receive regular pay, you mean.'

Don Quinn

`Yes, like everyone else who works a `job.'

Edward

`You got the bull by the horn.'

Don Quinn

'How do you mean?'

Edward

'Nobody wants to talk about the pay jazz workers receive.'

Don Quinn

'In terms of how much they make? It's embarrassing sometimes.'

Edward

'That's not the problem.'

Don Quinn

'So, what do we do?'

Edward

'A serious strategy is needed to address this problem. We need to refocus attention some place else.'

Don Quinn

'How do mean?'

Edward

'The churches!'

Don Quinn

'The churches. Black churches? You crazy, man.'

Edward

'And?'

Don Quinn

'Black people love good music. I mean music. They have not heard jazz.'

Edward

'And, the jazz musician does play good music.'

Don Quinn

'Excellent music.'

Edward

'The need to be in the churches.'

Don Quinn

'What about the community centers? And, white churches?'

Edward

'Hey, the music belongs to everybody, now. Sure, everywhere. That's what I mean. The black church is justa symbol. I want it to be in the forefront. A starting point.'

Don Quinn

'A base!'

Edward

'Yes, a base. That would be good. Yea, real good.'

Don Quinn

'What about the churches that are already doing it, do you discount them? Most are white you know?'

Edward

'Those that are doing it now will continue I suppose. The question is how do others do it. I am placing responsibility on the black churches because they have deliberately avoided jazz in their meeting halls. How does one avoid its greatest cultural contribution to find art? To world culture? To peace? A whole set of new aesthetics principles have been developed around this contribution.'

Don Quinn

'The question is, how do you do it?'

Edward

'Sponsor concerts in the churches.'

Don Quinn

'When? How?'

Edward

'Have all day Saturday workshops followed by concerts. Have fund raising to purchase instruments. Take advantage of the over supply of musicians. Give them jobs teaching instrumentation and vocal during the week days after school and on the weekend. Create contests as is already done for gospel music.'

DonQuinn

'Yea, sponsor concerts every Saturday, and then on Sunday afternoon. Open to the community.'

Edward

'Who would perform?'

Don Quinn

'The Masters would perform. Many could also serve as teachers.'

Edward

'Who would pay for this?'

Don Quinn

'A combination of resources. Church donations, corporate sponsors, the sky is the limit. What ever your imagination can conceive.'

Edward

'You're dreaming.'

Don Quinn

'Naw, it'll work. you must have faith.'

Edward

'Yea, but that will not replace the nite-clubs.'

Don Quinn

'That is not the intent.'

Edward

'To offer venues for creative music.'

Don Quinn

'Nothing else.'

Edward

'Breaking new ground for young, new musicians to receive first hand exposure to a great music tradition. I say duplicate the Junior Choirs at the Baptist and Church of God churches. You know how young people are, they will mimic what they see when it is fascinating. Place it in front of them and they will try it.'

Don Quinn

'Why the panic?'

Edward

'No panic, right now, at least. Our children are in need for consciousness building around their culture. They know nothing about their ancestors.'

Don Quinn

~Oh I agree, something needs to be done.'

Edward

`You never miss your water `til your well runs dry.'

Don Quinn

`Never!So, what's the problem to cause all of this excitement.'

Edward

`Apparently you did not hear me.Our youths are crying for attention.The fratricide has to end. Community centers will never serve enough of our youths to resolve that problem.'

Don Quinn

`Also, the musicians need a better support system.The work conditions have not really changed.In New York that it is.Other venues are needed because they offer the musicians better working conditions and pay for services rendered.Most have no health care, no retirement benefits.The list is endless.You would think that I am referring to the 1920's.'

Edward

`But isn't that how the free market works?'

Don Quinn

`No!Except for the most favored.The only democracy in the market place is for those who have.'

Edward

`Sure, but how do you correct it?'

Don Quinn

`You begin by examining the situation.'

Edward

`Okay?Have you done that?'

Don Quinn

`Yes.'

Edward

`And what did you find out?'

Don Quinn

`I found out that most of the jazz musicians who I talked to would qualify for welfare easily.These persons often have college degrees I am talking about.With their talents detected elsewhere, they would definitely make more money.'

Edward

`But isn't that explained by the theory on human capital in terms of opportunity costs.'

Don Quinn

`What?'

Edward

`Opportunity costs mean how much are you willing to invest in your future monetary gains.'

Don Quinn

`Well, that does not sound to reasonable. Musicians invest as much time, energy, and monetary resources into their professional development as a medical doctor. What is the point?'

Edward

`Yes, but you better know that when you make your investment. You know that when you make that decision you must live with it.'

Don Quinn

`I do not agree with that. At some point an advanced society must/should want to support its arts as a means of cultural continuity. In some hope of aesthetic redemption.'

Edward

`You are speaking of a welfare state, socialism.'

Don Quinn

`They are not the same.'

Edward

`What?'

Don Quinn

`They are not the same.'

Edward

`Oh! What is the difference?'

Don Quinn

`One is capitalism operating under the banner of social responsibility. That's the welfare state.'

Edward

`And, the other?'

Don Quinn

'Socialism. No one since the Native Peoples of the Americas has practiced that in this part of the world.'

Edward

'What about communist Russia?'

Don Quinn

'I take it you mean the Union of Soviet Socialist Republics. What about them? They certainly were not socialist. More like state welfare under a strictly authoritarian system. But that's a digression. Our concern is with the jazz musician.'

Edward

'So what are you talking about?'

Don Quinn

'I am referring to an advanced technological society regardless of socio-economic arrangement. I do not care what you call it, there is no need for practicing professionals to suffer illnesses because of the health care policy that offers no health care to its citizens and other residents.'

Edward

'That is going against the grain. However, it is unconscionable.'

Don Quinn

'Really. All of this goes back to the beginning with Africans being brought to America.'

Edward

'As slaves.'

Don Quinn

'Not all Africans were slaves. All were never slaves. However, that's another discussion. The point is Africans came from a world of music and ceremonies.'

Edward

'HA! HA! HA! AH! HA! Is that why we like to party? HA! HA!

Don Quinn

'It has to be. You mean with music. We dance, eat lots of food, drink a lot of booze, and play our music so everybody can hear it.'

Edward

'You mean loud and long, all night long.'

51

Don Quinn

'Well, some people seem to think so.'

Edward

'Those are the ones who are not usually at the party.'

Don Quinn

'That's the difference between a black party and a white party.'

Edward

'What happen?'

Don Quinn

'They don't have any music.'

Edward

'And, no food. That wine, sodas, orange juice, cheese and bread cuisine. My wife and I walked into a party, looked around and listened for the music. The host -- I use host for everybody whose giving something -- came over and I said, 'when's the party gone begin? Where's the music?'

Don Quinn

'They said, 'it's already going on why'd you ask?'

Edward

'I said, without music? She looked at me in amazement. It never occurred to her to place some music on the stereo because she was throwing a party.'

Don Quinn

'What did she do?'

Edward

'She said, go play some.'

Don Quinn

'I hear you.'

Edward

'Now, what was I saying. Uh! Oh yes, about the Africans coming over as musicians and bringing their instruments with them.'

Don Quinn

'During slavery.'

Edward

'Yes, sure, of course. There was never any real respect shown for those primitive instruments by the white settler population, except the banjo.'

Don Quinn

'Be careful with that.'

Edward

'What do you mean?'

Don Quinn

'First, they could not bring any instruments over when they were fitted in the bottom of the ship like sardines. Second, they did not have to, and ...'

Edward

'...Third?...'

Don Quinn

'...Third, the banjo was not the only instrument retained, copied and modified.'

Edward

'Name another.'

Don Quinn

'Xylophone. Marimba.'

Edward

Oh, I never thought about that instrument.'

Don Quinn

'Many plantations had some band of some sorts. They were there to entertain the niggers.'

Edward

'And the white folks, too.'

Don Quinn

'The plantocracy.'

Edward

'What?'

Don Quinn

'They entertained the plantocracy, too.'

Edward

'How was that?I was told that they took all of our instruments away from us.Especially the drum.'

Don Quinn

'That is true, but only partially.The taking of the drum in black mythology about slavery is more symbolic than actual.'

Edward

'What are you saying?That they did not take away the drum?'

Don Quinn

'Sure they did.They took away the drum, but that did not stop communication from going on.The plantation owner and the overseer misunderstood the role of the drum.'

Edward

'What do you mean?The talking drum could send messages.'

Don Quinn

'That was not the only role of to drum.'

Edward

'What other role did it play?'

Don Quinn

'Rhythm.The rhythm that some plantation owners detested because the women and men would gyrate sensuously, did not need a drum.It was inherent in the people.Anything could become a drum.That was easy. The slaves simply translated their conspiracies to singing and lyrics.No problem.'

Edward

'They continued the practice in another form.'

Don Quinn

'Exactly.'

Edward

'The mistake was not in realizing that the slave came from all parts of Africa.The ones who came from the Northwest interior and further east made and played string instruments.Others brought with them other ways of making music.Remember that the slaves came from as far as

Don Quinn

Mozambique and Angola to Mali, Mauritania, Chad, and Bekina Faso. Remember the Moors left what we know today as Flamenco today in Spain. Like Lightning' Hopkins said, `1000 years of slavery' had made us adaptable. So we brought the music in our heads with us.'

Edward

`Black-a-Moors they were called. I agree. You can see it in Cuba, Haiti and Trinidad, and Brazil. But I fail to see it in the African American.'

Don Quinn

`Sure you can. You simply have to look at it differently. Ask different questions.'

Edward

`You mean the base. The starting point.'

Don Quinn

`Yes, it's always European. Everything is done from a European perspective. Never any attempt to learn how the other people explain themselves.'

Edward

`Like Japan, you mean?'

Don Quinn

`Exactly! Same results.'

Edward

`Well, not quite.'

Don Quinn

`Yes, you are right. The Japanese have a power relationship with Europe and North America that is different. They hang with the G7 group. They operate as equals.'

Edward

`Americans are at a loss to explain how that happened.'

Don Quinn

`That comes from being ignorant about other cultures, other societies.'

Edward

`Wrong base!'

Don Quinn

'They explain everything including aesthetics from their own perspective.

Edward

'Own knowledge base.'

Don Quinn

'Other's cultural variables are not understood as these cultures intend them to be. This causes great errors of judgment about what the motives of others are.'

Edward

'That even applies to its own society.'

Don Quinn

'What do you mean?'

Edward

'Jazz.'

Don Quinn

'Jazz. Ain't that nothing. A word equivalent to 'nigger,' 'dread,' and 'bitch' is the official name of America's art music.'

Edward

'You mean Jazz? What's in a name?'

Don Quinn

'The basis of a claim.'

Edward

'The basis of a clam.'

Don Quinn

'That 's what's in a name.'

Edward

'It's like dreadlocks.'

Don Quinn

'How do you mean? I lost you on that one.'

56

Edward

'Dread.What does dread mean?'

Don Quinn

'Evil! Oh yes, I see.Dread Lock. HA! HA! They get us every time.At every turn.'

Edward

'Always with a negative interpretation.'

Don Quinn

'Like the word culture.We are not American culture, we are a 'sub-culture' within the American culture.'

Edward

'The white man.A sub-culture. HUH!Sound like a joke to me.'

Don Quinn

'Yes, of course. That is who we are talking about all of the time.'

Edward

'Does that mean that we have an under culture?African Americans are an under culture. HA HA. HA! HA!'

Don Quinn

'So, you live in the underworld.'

Edward

'HA! HA! You?You mean us, just us.For members only.You are in this mess too.And we didn't even know what they were saying about us to our faces.Gots to give it to them.They did it at every turn.Words. They used words.HA! HA! HA!

Don Quinn

'Language.Our music is our language.That's why we've got to bring the music into the churches.'

Edward

'I know.The kids would love it.But it won't happen unless we see white people do it. Now, that's who you gotta see.'

Don Quinn

'Who you have to sell.'

Edward

'Phew!There is a core.It is small, but it is dedicated, and in place.'

Don Quinn

`We simply must strengthen and broaden it.'

Edward

`The base.'

Don Quinn

`We've got to treat our music like European music is treated.It's nurtured and protected.'

Edward

`Let's not overstate this support.Although by comparison it is rich versus poor.'

Don Quinn

`That's hard to take.'

Edward

`What's that?'

Don Quinn

`Seeing our own inventors live by their wits to survive.'

Edward

`While the tax payers pay for the philharmonics, opera houses, and ballet companies.'

Don Quinn

`And, museums that have none of our works on display.There is no parity.'

Edward

`Be careful with that.Africa is well represented in the major museums among the G7 group.Don't make your focus so narrow. The entire European Community and North America.

DonQuinn

`I know Africa is represented in many forms within the museum's culture of collecting.Its collections are often strong on African representations of civilizations and empires, but I guess I suffer from that same old divide and conquer syndrome.'

Edward

`What do you mean?'

Don Quinn

`I still think in terms of where we live not any place else.'

Edward

'Be careful with that.'

Don Quinn

'Yea, I know, but it's hard to get rid of old habits, old ways of thinking.Still, I say that there must be fairness.Fairness is the only way to be fair. Things are very unfair.'

Edward

'Fairness.It comes to us in the market place that we are suppose to respond to.The most favored have us to tax for their pleasures and entertainment.'

Don Quinn

'Right out of 1984.Double talk.'

Edward

'I think that's double speak, not double talk.The native people called it forked tongue.'

Don Quinn

'Du Bois called it double life.Present day scholars call it duality.They even say that's what Du Bois called it. The term seems more modern than 1900.'

Edward

'But that 's what it means.'

Don Quinn

'Of course!'

Edward

'That is the specific contradiction reserved for people of color, the other side of double talk.'

Don Quinn

'What is the specific contradiction reserved for people of color?

Edward

Double talk?Double speak?Double life?What?'

Don Quinn

'It means that we operate within two worlds simultaneously.'

Edward

'Acomplementarities of sorts.'

Don Quinn

'A what?'

Edward

'The black world is simultaneously a duality that operates in complementarities with the white world.'

Don Quinn

'Are you shit-tin' me?'

Edward

'HA! HA! AH! HA!'

Don Quinn

~For real.'

Edward

'I knew you were shit-tin' me. That ain't for real. What you said can't be for real. I didn't understand one thing you said.'

Don Quinn

'So it cannot be for real?'

Edward

'Ain't no way.'

Don Quinn

'Then, explain how we standing here talking about if it ain't for real as you say.'

Edward

'Cause don't nobody talk that way....Use those words, but people who ain't for real. So, I know what you say ain't for real.'

Don Quinn

'HA! HA! AH! AH! HA!'

Edward

'That's funny. What you just said is funny. Com-ple-men-tar-i-es si-mul-tan-e-ous-lies, du-al-ity. A duality is simultaneously in complementarities. That is the black man's contradiction. It damn show is. And, he'll never git out of it 'cause he cain't even pronounce it. HA! HA! HA! HA! He don't even know what it is, he's living two lives for.'

60

Don Quinn

`We are speaking in the future-present.'

Edward

`The what? Where do you..?'

Don Quinn

`Duality as double speak is the future-present. What you are speaking about now is in the future-present.'

Edward

`Oh, I am. I always thought that its only the present and the future is hereafter. You know, like in heaven or hell.'

Don Quinn

`We are speaking of futurist. When a futurist like Du Bois speaks of the future, he is speaking about the future-present. The after now.'

Edward

`You mean that you can see it right now right in front of you?'

Don Quinn

`Yes, of course. That's it.'

Edward

`Give me an example.'

Don Quinn

`Yes, back to the double speak. Double speak tells you that there is fairness practiced when old European music is classical; that classical music is art music and Jazz is `pop' music' but not art music, too.'

Edward

`Sure, look at them.'

Don Quinn

`Fairness becomes the twin of the disadvantaged. That is, they operate...'

Edward

`...Simultaneously.'

Don Quinn

`Exactly.'

61

Edward

`The language can be very confusing to those trying to enter the mainstream.It can become very confusing.'

Don Quinn

`I could not have said it better.The disadvantaged in the United States are its indigenous art forms.To show that they are disadvantaged, the art is referred to as `folk' art.There is art and there is folk art.'

Edward

`And, pop art.'

Don Quinn

`What is folk art?'

Edward

`Damn if I know.Something about people whoso cultures have not been exposed to European ways of life.When Europeans discover these people and their art they call them and their art primitive.A polite way of saying primitive is to call it folk, folk art.'

Don Quinn

`All of this seems to stem from the least favored principle.Country blues is folk, New Orleans `jaazzz' is pop.'

Edward

`Each music is severely disadvantaged because it originates from the least favored people in society.'

Don Quinn

`This music is revered and the people who create it are despised and spited by members who dominate the cultural and artistic values in the U.S.'

Edward

`And, black music is treated accordingly.'

Don Quinn

`True.But, not completely.The dominance is not complete.'

Edward

`Nearly.'

Don Quinn

`Look at music.'

'Which music?Pop music?Classical music?'

Don Quinn

'No!African American Art Music.America's art music.That is certainly from the least favored.This is the most profound and original contribution to world aesthetics from this culture.'

Edward

'And, in this century.'

Don Quinn

'Well, it certainly does dominate world popular music.'

Edward

'But neither Blues or jazz is treated with the respect it would receive if a Gershwin were its inventor.And, if musicians from the most favored were it celebrated geniuses.'

Don Quinn

'Unfortunately, they are not.'

Edward

'Because they are not its inventors, the music is treated like a minor art with no aesthetic base.At least not one that is as generational, that is, its heritage is not as long, as the one promoted as American art music.'

Don Quinn

'The fraud is unfortunate.'

Edward

'Is it?'

Don Quinn

'Well, being treated as a minor art with questionable pedigree.'

Edward

'Of questionable aesthetic value?'

Don Quinn

'Yes.'

Edward

'I would say that it is more serious than unfortunate.'

Don Quinn

'You say that it is American's art music, but the most favored say that it is pop music.'

Edward

'They are the greater population.And, they have no obligation to give us credit for 'their' music.'

Don Quinn

'The thing is being the most favored always gives you an advantage when something great is accomplished. Anything successful means that you benefit because it is automatically assumed that this is a creation of the majority unless otherwise reported.'

Edward

'The key is otherwise reported.'

Don Quinn

'Some artists make it in-spite of this lack of respect and honesty on the part of the most favored.'

Edward

'Yea, and if they get rich enough,...

Don Quinn

'...You become an honorary most favored.'

Edward

'If someone is looking for African Americans who cannot claim disadvantage look at the multi-rich. Especially those who have celebrity status.'

Don Quinn

'I know what you mean.It is this special group who can claim that they don't suffer any discrimination. And, be factual about it.'

Edward

'No disadvantage.'

Don Quinn

'None!The question is can they pass this honorary position on to their off-spring?'

Edward

'No!'

Don Quinn

'Why not?The Japanese have done it in Peru, South Africa,...'

64

Edward

'...But that's a whole 'noth-er discussion. I think that for the disadvantaged who represent the least favored have no permanent claim on any spot of the most favored position.'

Don Quinn

'Nor does anyone else.'

Edward

'For individuals, that is true. It is another thing for the group. The group always remains virtually the same. Individuals may come and go but the group never changes. That is the difference. Same for the least favored position.'

Don Quinn

'Why?'

Edward

'The position is institutionalized, and custom has not made any great effort to remove it.'

Don Quinn

'How so?'

Edward

'Race color. Color race. Whatever. Sinister concept. As long as no one will admit to the black blood running in their veins we will always suffer a disadvantage from being the least favored because we openly come from the black, the slave, the negro, so-called.'

Don Quinn

'What we agree saying here is that creative musicians who come from the least favored will more often than not suffer a disadvantage.' Oh...?

Edward

'In the market place.'

Don Quinn

'Definitely within the market place! There more so than any other place. The market place is the last place creative musicians need to be.'

Edward

'I think that you should distinguish between the aesthetic market place and the economic market place. Creativity is the last thing the players look for in the economic market place. It is the first thing they look for in the aesthetic market place. That is the only way you really make a name for yourself among your peers. You must meet their standard of excellence. There's it the only one that counts.'

Don Quinn

`Until you start bringing in that bread. Then what?'

Edward

`If you are creative like Miles Davis, and marketable so much the better. Money is the bottom line. That's why they will have a black singer make a record and never release it. They want your voice under the most favorable conditions so that they can let a white singer study it, learn how to sing it good enough to sell, because white buyers will buy it sooner than if the black singer had released it first. The A&R people want their buying customers to think that the origin of that music is white. The list is endless.'

Don Quinn

`Yea, they still doing it! I heard, let's see, who was it, any way, there was this black singer who just said that the other day on one of them talk shows. Damn, I wish I could remember who it was? Oh, yes, Ruth Brown.'

Edward

`I thought you were going to say La Verne Baker.'

Don Quinn

HA! HA! I thought you were going to say Gladys Knight.'

Edward

`Yea, that's her. Damn, couldn't think of that for nothing. Ain't that some shit. Couldn't think of Gladys Knight and the Pips. Must be getting old.'

Don Quinn

`Right, You just ain't gots no brain.'

Edward

`Now, we don't even need to go there. We talking about something important now. No need for the bull shit.'

Don Quinn

`Sorry!"

Edward

`The point from that conversation is, will the consumer buy the product?' Will she purchase the product?'

Don Quinn

`Creative labor. The whole thing is about creative labor. There can be no value in the product without creative labor.'

Edward

'Are you talking about creative energy? Is that the same thing?'

Don Quinn

'Yes, it is through the labor process that one is rewarded for the end product. In jazz the audience prefers to see you make your product right before them. That is what makes it unique. The jazz audience wants to see what the performers are doing tonight. Am I going to hear something new, this evening? You know what I mean?'

Edward

'Does it affect their music?

Don Quinn

'Not receiving the value of the labor you invested is always a hard thing to accept.'

Edward

'Yea, for the creative musicians, they seem to hang in there.'

Don Quinn

'I agree, but for this generation the word is not in yet on what new value they have offered to the development of this artistic music. Only a very few are approaching making a new statement. The ones that you can hear, I mean. The blackout on the more innovative ones is going to keep the development stale like a pond devoid of fresh water. I know that there have to be some new voices out there. There always has been. I hope they do not get lost in this formalization of what constitutes jazz music.'

Edward

'You don't mean that the music is dying do you?'

Don Quinn

'In terms of entropy?'

Edward

'In what? Why do you do that? Every time we try to have conversation you pull them big words out on me. Why?'

Don Quinn

'Well, didn't somebody say that this system is closed to the least favored?'

Edward

'I have said that before. I stand by that. But nothin' is absolute here. The system is not absolute, at least not as absolute as it might be in South Africa or Zimbabwe or Brazil. The systems are closed there. I cannot say that with completeness here.'

Don Quinn

'Yes, but look at the price. They do manage to rise above the system, but no one is ready to reward them for their efforts.'

Edward

'Cynic.'

Don Quinn

'Skeptic.'

Edward

'Maybe, but...'

Don Quinn

Many of the new generation musicians are very profitable with their music business.'

Edward

'I guess something has to suffer.'

Don Quinn

'What do you mean?'

Edward

'Your livelihood or your art.'

Don Quinn

'Musicians must become business oriented.'

Edward

'Many are as I pointed out. They may qualify for grants and other forms of subsidy. That is not very many however.'

Don Quinn

'Is that why you say that the music is becoming too one dimensional? Jazz I mean?'

Edward

'Everything seems to be headed toward conformity. There is some good music out there. Nothing like the 1970's. Not even like the 1950's and 60's, although this is where the renaissance has come from. No Cecil Taylor, Ornette Coleman, John Coltrane, and that crowd. No Art Ensemble. Sun Ra.'

Don Quinn

`Marvin `Hanibal' Petersons, Ronald Shannon Jackson, Keith Jarrett, Dewey Redman, Freddie Hubbard, Joe Henderson, Andrew Cyrille.

Edward

`Yea, his son don't quite make it.It least not in the same class with the guy who played with Keith Jarrett. That's how I feel.'

Don Quinn

`Ain't nobody said nothing.'

Edward

`Yea, but I know you dudes.'

Don Quinn

`Creative musicians do not enjoy the luxury of a school teacher or social worker.The get no benefits. They must save their own money, what little they get, so most don't retire.'

Edward

`You must understand, musicians are different people.They approach the world differently.'

Don Quinn

`What are they? HA! HA! HA! `

Edward

{Ignoring question as though rhetorical.}

Don Quinn

`You are right.Musicians do need support.'

Edward

`The problem is they are attached to an ignored aesthetic.'

Don Quinn

`No one wants to acknowledge the labor process that goes into producing this music everyone insists on calling jazz.Only creative labor performed as human capital can produce anything original or creative.I cannot see a machine adding value to a piece like A LOVE SUPREME by John Coltrane.'

Edward

`Is your contention that there could be no jazz without creative labor?'

69

Don Quinn

`Yes, none that I can imagine.Creative labor is a human endeavor.The creative effort is to communicate with the audience.A jazz concert is an event.The performance sis an activity engaged in through a labor process called creativity.'

Edward

`Why are you emphasizing the labor process so much?'

Don Quinn

`Jazz differs from other western musical forms in that it is suppose to always be a work in progress.Ever changing.Never the same. It is not the score that is suppose to determine the process. It is more like serving as a guide and points of reference, departure and reentry. And that is not always present.When a form is supplied, the musicians performing the piece must labor to invent and discover how they are going to make the music interesting, exciting and true to the form developed by the arranger.

Edward

`I see it more as a relationship to the audience you are performing for. It is not an object that can be viewed like a painting.It must be recorded aurally to be heard over and over like one sees a painting everyday. The listener is searching for its perfection and continuity of development as the musician moves you toward the end of the performance.The performance always comes to an end.'

Background Ease Dropper

Better tell that to Cecil Taylor, Sun Ra and John Coltrane.Laughter.] {Continues as though nothing was said}

`Don Quinn

`Of course assuming this posture, jazz musicians are subject to open mistakes.'

Edward

`Exactly, but it is the natural sound that I look for in a musician. I want to hear his or her sound coming through.Every musician must develop a sound that belongs to them.You can improvise all you want but if you don't have your own sound, you begin to sound indistinguishable from someone else.That's bad.'

Don Quinn

`What do you mean?'

Edward

`You know what I mean.I can tell it is Anee Sharon Freeman as soon as I hear her voice, piano voice I mean.I can tell it is Gerry Eastman every time I hear him on guitar.Same thing with Jann Parker and Talib Kibwe, a.k.a, T.K.Blue. I have a problem when it comes to the 1980's youth.I find it difficult to tell whose who.'

Don Quinn

`I know what you mean.I thought it was just me.'

Edward

`There are some voices that stand out.'

Don Quinn

`Like who?'

Edward

`Steve Coleman. Teri Lynne Carrington, Roy Hargrove. Geri Allen, Phillip Harper. Cyrus Chessnut, Casandra Wilson,....

Don Quinn

`But jazz is a commodity.Remember the market place.'

Edward

`That is exactly what I am talking about.With jazz a musician must have a voice and musical approach that is unique to that person.That person only.'

Don Quinn

`The question is, what are the patrons buying?The music or the musician?'

Edward

`Can jazz be jazz apart from it creator?Mozart's scores can be played by others but is that Mozart?Why do they attempt to play Mozart?Play Mozart's music the way you feel it, the way you would like to play if you had arranged it. Only Mozart can play Mozart. Only Cecil Taylor is Cecil Taylor.Only Jackie McLean is Jackie McLean.The musical equations although exact, because they are exact, will never allow you to play Mozart, unless you want to play it by rote, after recording the sound of his performance, and attempting to play it exactly the way you hear Mozart hears Mozart. That looses Mozart right there.There is nothing creative about that.Machines can be programmed to do that. Music is only original once.With spontaneous composition being the ultimate in a masterful jazz performance, forcing jazz artists to sanitize their music to suit the ears of the A&R personnel so that they may be recorded, promoted and have their music distributed, the contradiction is, do I sellout or can I remain an artist and make me some money?'

Don Quinn

`Can't he do both?' Or, she, excuse me, women play jazz, too.We forget that a lot. But...'

Edward

`...Can't they do both?'

71

Don Quinn

'Yes, but it's hard. Some can, some find the money too much to resist, often saying, now I can play what I want, when I want. Only to find out that the decision is no longer theirs to make.'

Edward

'Some really cannot play jazz, but can sound like they are playing jazz. They are not usually good at improvising.'

Don Quinn

'They are good at advertising. CD101 FM.'

Edward

'Only WKCR plays the real stuff. That shit you don't hear no where else.'

Don Quinn

'Your comment about the ability to play this music is right on time. That is so true. But is it not the same way in the movie industry and the theatre?'

Edward

'For the regular public there is no difference in what we call jazz and what is being sold as jazz. It is like the silver screen and theatre. It's all the same. They like it. They like CD101 FM and they like the silver screen. All of this stuff we are discussing now is totally irrelevant to them. Their concern is, does it sound the way I like to hear it? Was the film entertaining?'

Don Quinn

'I don't know about that. In reference to that statement about Mozart and creativity. I heard Gary Bartz one night and swore that I was listening to Coltrane playing alto. But you knew it was not Coltrane. And it was creative, it was Gary doing his version of Coltrane. It had that special feel that only Coltrane could give.'

Edward

'Like Steve Reid the drummer with Charles Tyler.'

Don Quinn

'Who?'

Edward

'The drummer. He played with Miles Davis on the Tu Tu CD. I thought that I was listening to Ed Blackwell. But it didn't sound like Ed Blackwell after I heard more. The likeness was his approach to time and rhythm.'

Don Quinn

'You mean Steve Reid. Like Andrew White, a musician who translated Coltrane's works.'

Edward

'Transcribed.'

Don Quinn

'Yea.'

Edward

'I bet he sound like a Coltrane clone.'

Don Quinn

'No on the contrary, he had his own very interesting sound and style.Definitely his own voice.Oh, it was obvious that he had learned at Coltrane University. No doubt.But this was Andrew White with the Julius Hemphill sextet of saxophones.SnugHarbor Staten Island is where I saw him.' Like Odean Pope!

Edward

'That is what you said.You can't divorce jazz from the performer.The music is the performer.The music is in the performance.The performers are the music creators.'

Don Quinn

'That's true.That also brings up another point.'

Edward

'What's that?'

Don Quinn

'In its resurgence, there were those who contend that new wave jazz has lost its creativity due to its insistence on intensity.That this intensity is boring because it is mediocre.Unoriginal.

Edward

'They are not saying anything new, we say.'

Don Quinn

'They are not saying anything, we say.'

Edward

'Yea,...' [Trying to get a word in edge wise.]

Don Quinn

'...Hold up.Hold up. Let me finish.Neither the mainstream or the most favored are willing to embrace it.'

Edward

'Well, I hear that the problem is, musicians have bought into commercialism. The contradiction is more apparent when those who want to work within the market place challenge those who treat the music as an art.'

Don Quinn

'The problem is not as simple as you are putting it. It cannot be divided so easily as A&R people controlling the market place. They tried to pigeon hold 'black music.' It did not work because American popular music is black music. Somebody thought that they could make white musicians pop musicians and black musicians black musicians. White music is black music. Black music is white music. Pop music is black music usually sung by white singers and performed by white bands as white music. What a fraud. We would be hanged from a tree if we stole as much from them as they steal from us.'

Edward

'I hear yea. The problem is, so many musicians have bought into that Kenny G playing that they have no voice we can identify. That form of commercialism becomes additive. Really, David Sanborn.'

Don Quinn

'The only problem is if you are lucky, you may get one hit, then what? Concerts where the only tune you are expected to perform is the hit. That can become a problem,'

Edward

'Do black musicians have a choice?'

Don Quinn

'Yes! No! If they want to be commercial, they don't have a choice.'

Edward

'If they don't want to be commercial, they have a problem getting a recording contract.'

Don Quinn

'What are good musicians to do?'

Edward

'If they want to pursue degrees and learn other areas, they have a choice. Jazz musicians need to learn the entire business. There is no rule that says creativity and ignorance would go together.'

Don Quinn

'That reminds me of the black colleges.'

Edward

'The lack of jazz programs. That has always been a sore spot with me.'

Don Quinn

`How do you mean?'

Edward

`I have yet to accept the fact that black colleges rejected jazz on their campuses.'

Don Quinn

`Do not be a-historical, now.'

Edward

`What was the problem?It seems so natural. They had first claim as the place where black culture would be taught and retained.'

Don Quinn

`They did the opposite.They ran the other way.'

Edward

`That is a very apolitical statement.'

Don Quinn

`Until those students took over the colleges in the 1960's and 70's.Student revolutions all over the place.'

Edward

`They did not develop jazz programs for a while after that.It was the generation of students I attended college who made the changes. Put in new jazz programs.

Don Quinn

`Those are very few.Under ten I think.'

Edward

`Shameful.'

Don Quinn

`Do not get doctrinaire now.Understand the politics of the South.Freedom was very limited.'

Edward

`Apologist?Now I see your stripes.'

Don Quinn

`Say what you want, there are more white colleges that offer majors in jazz than black colleges.I find that difficult to understand when these same colleges could support an orchestra that learned European music as a major....Could get a major in music and music education without ever offering one course in black music, not even jazz, a highly respected art form in Europe by the time we entered college. To add insult to injury they maintained an a capella choir that sang spirituals and European choir music.'

Edward

'Inferiority.'

Don Quinn

'No, that is being very naive. The conservative nature of most presidents and their inability to raise money made them vulnerable to the politicians who were never interested in the education of black youth. There are many programs that were never born because of the precarious situation the institutions were always in financially. That problem of degrees was not an exclusive thing for jazz, many things took a back seat.'

Edward

'Sure! Acceptance was the ideal state to be realized. It was very important to be received as equals.'

Don Quinn

'You mean be on one of those, one of my best friends list'

Edward

'Jesus, you are so cynical.'

Don Quinn

'It's humorous to me.'

Edward

'They claimed that they could not understand jazz.'

Don Quinn

'Or, jazz musicians were drug addicts.'

Edward

'Or, it was no better than the blues.'

Don Quinn

'Meaning low life.'

Edward

'Even worse. The drugs.'

Don Quinn

'Narcotics.Just the very name brought fear and silence.'

Edward

'It wasn't legitimate.Classical was.'

Don Quinn

Things have changed now.It hurts that it was a segregated university, North Texas State...

Edward

'...University of North Texas....'

Don Quinn

'That offered the first degree in jazz studies. 1938.

Edward

'This had long since changed. Billy Harper graduated there.'

Don Quinn

'Yes, but no Texas University that is black has a degree.'

Edward

'You can take it in music education.They consider that the same thing.Not only that, the bands always played jazz, even at the football games.'

Don Quinn

'Yea, yea, I know.'

Edward

'Interesting that musicians like Dewey Redman graduated from one of those black colleges in Texas.I think it was Prairie View.'

Don Quinn

'Dewey Redman, Prairie View.Now he's bad.Some of the most beautiful improvisations in music.'

Edward

'Well, the white scholars have done no better.It has taken Europeans like Charles Delacnay, Hugues Panassie, and Robert Coffin probably created more discographies than any of the American writers.It is a process that is a fine art in Europe today.They still have the finest lists of names of jazz musicians across the world as you can find anywhere.'

Don Quinn

`These were the first jazz scholars that you are speaking of?'

Edward

`We really need more African American scholars studying black music, especially jazz.'

Don Quinn

`All music!'

Edward

`All music, especially music of African, Asia, and the Americas.'

Don Quinn

`It is called audience development.'

Edward

`A natural base and they do not know what our musicians are doing.'

Don Quinn

`The thing is the students love the music when they hear it.'

Edward

`The technique is easy.Start them early, in kindergarten is the place to start teaching them music.'

Don Quinn

`With no program, there are enough students at the colleges to start programs with the young children. They use to be in high school bands.The process does not require very much.Some home made instruments.A little love and attention.Some praise.'

Edward

`I understand that, but music is our life blood.Our music expresses it like no other.Something must be done to save that element of our music.It keeps all of the other things about us going.It just seems so wrong for a world art to receive so little attention at home.The word is, a hero has to be accepted else where before there will be recognition at home.And, only maybe, then.'

Don Quinn

`Well, isn't it about time that we pay homage by institutionalizing our training process.Music keeps us going.Yet, we give back to it so unevenly.'

Edward

`And, to the wrong people.It's like we really don't understand.'

Don Quinn

'We really don't. We don't.

Edward

'Why?'

Don Quinn

'Too many distractions like racism, survival, the bogey man.'

Edward

'Yes, but, there seems to be more interest in black music than ever before. I have not been to a jazz concert in a public location that was not full. The interest is there. That's why we must seize the time. The time is now.'

Don Quinn

'Now's the time. HA! HA! HA! HA! [Everybody slap hands and split.]

[Charlie Parker can be heard playing his composition 'Now's The Time.']

THE END

ON CRITICISM
delridge l. hunter
[Please read aloud]

The Jazz Worker
The jazz worker is creative,
Thoughtful,
An observer,
A provider of musical ideas,
As one continues thought.

A student of sound that sings blue,
Make song into sound that is rings true.

Seldom ever rewarded the money
Commensurate with the talent

Characters
Scatman
Koo kat
Off Beat
Barbershop Quartet
'Round 'Bout

Aesthetics. Aesthetics is a philosophical term coined by Alexander Baumgartner in 1735. Aesthetics now denotes the philosophical problems raised regarding the creative labor (energy) that results in the creation of fine arts. As this definition applies to music, aesthetics examines issues of a philosophical character surrounding music as an art form. Aesthetics evolved as James Harris once said, because `music [is] at best...an imperfect art.'James Harris. 1744. DISCOURSE ON MUSIC, PAINTING AND POETRY. London. As an imperfect art, the creative labor interacts with and reflects the cultural background of the creators of art and its respondents.

Criticism. Criticism sheds light on and interprets a work (i.e., literary, composed, or artistic) and performance (i.e., dance, drama, or musical) as demonstrated. What is illuminated (i.e., the critique) is based on the experience and knowledge of an informed individual. The informed individual, called critic, informs what the creative worker demonstrated rather than attempt to discover how it was done.

[While Bitches Brew by Miles Davis is playing in the background, the barbershop critics are engaged in their usual discussions on who's who and what's what.]

Scatman:

YO! Blood what's happenin'?Why you gots to be playin' dat lame shit by dat traitor

80

Miles

Davls.I stopped listenin' to his shit after the European concert with George Coleman,

Herbie Hancock, Tony Williams, and Ron Carter.You remember, Coleman did this wild solo as classic as Paul Gonzales did with Ellington, the Duke.It was bad, I mean baad. [Slap five, Right On!]Anything after dat is pure de bull shit.Tak' my word.

Kool Kat

I can dig it.But, I like Miles.What ever he do, I buy it.He's still the man.You just don't know nothin,' new, different.You old.

[Everybody laughs]

Scatman

Old my ass.You the ole' one.You old.Yea, I...

Off Beat

YO! Why don't yawl stop that nonsense.You both is old.Older than sweat.Smell like it too.

Kool Kat

Look whose talkin'.Man, you older than dirt.Matter of fact, you look so old they removed you from old age pension and gave you a new birth certificate.

[By now, the place is rolling with laughter.]

Scatman

Yea, you so old dat time stopped when it came upon your number.

[The barbershop begins to rock with laughter.The laughter begins to sound like a quarter with all of the singing and shouting going on inside.]

Off Beat

Yea, Yea, yea.Alright, but check this out.

[The whole barbershop roars again, then dies down for Off Beat to speak.But before,..]

Barbershop Quartet

UH! HUH! Here we go.Grab yo seats boys Off Beat is about to give us the latest shit on the planet Earth.

81

Barbershop Solo

From the world of the intellectuals. HA! HA! HA! HA!.

Off Beat

Ah'right, yawl.I ain't tellin' you shit. NAW!Yawl don't want to hear nothin' but whose doin' it to who.And, what little girl yawl want to hit on if you was just...

Barbershop Quartet

...young as we was thirty years ago. [Everybody laughs.]Naw man.You know we was

teasin.' Go on.What's new out there?Tell us about them jazz scholars.What they

sayin' now?

Off Beat

Well, I was reading...

[Noticing Off Beat's change in language.]

Scat Man

Check dis, Off Beat's `bout to git into his academic mode.

[Barbershop Quartet (BQ) laughs with approval.They get a kick out of Off Beat being able to change from the folks way of speaking to how they sound downtown.]

Off Beat

I was reading this criticism of jazz by Ted Gioia and in it he said that it is by historic accident that jazz has black origins.

BQ

Say what?

Kool Kat

I'm sure he believes that Earth is a historical accident.(Pause) Where he git comin' off with some shit like that?Whose this mutha, Off Beat?Just give me his name.

Off Beat

I do not have a problem with that.It's the part where he contends that it might have been someone else outside the African frame.That the cultural elite might just as well have made such an invention.

82

Kool Kat

Say what?

Scatman

What is this shit based on?

BQ

Does he believe in Jesus Christ?

Kool Kat

Why yawl ask dat?

Scatman

J.C. came from the least favored.

BQ

[Singing/rapping] HA! HA! HA! HA! AH! HA! HA! AFRICAN AMERICANS THE LEAST FAVORED SIMPLY ACT AS HOSTS TO THIS MUSIC THEY COME BY HISTORIC ACCIDENT. HA! HA! HA!

Kool Kat

Jazz started out by historical accident. HA! HA!

Off Beat

I can understand the idea that it could have been invented in other places African Americans lived and performed in, but someone from the cultural elite....

Scatman

Just how many masterpieces have come from the cultural elite? How many invention in music? In America today?

Off Beat

It is called the most favored position thesis.

Kool Kat

 How this come up?

[Speaking to the original point on the floor]

83

Off Beat

I wondered that same thing to, when I read it. I said, `why would he say something racist like dat? What is his motive?'

BQ Solo

Provocation!

BQ RSVP

Show off.

BQ Baritone

Ignorance.

BQ RSVP

Show off.

Scatman

Tryin' to show everybody how deep he is.

Round `Bout

I heard somebody try to apply that same thesis to Africa. That by historical accident Africa is the birth place of society, everybody human.

Kool Kat

Damn man, you always put things different. I thought you were going to say mankind or something like that, and...

Scatman

...He said, `people and society.' I can dig it.

Off Beat

Because that is what we are. People constitute society. A social organization is made up of intelligent beings.

Kool Kat

There he goes again. I think `a society' and he says a social organization.

Scatman

ANYWAY!

Off Beat

Anyway, I found it so odd that a critic would say that except to attract attention to his title.

Kool Kat

What was the title

Off Beat

IMPERFECT ART.The imperfect art.But, check this, he calls jazz an imperfect art with a questionable aesthetic.

Round `Bout

That's some bold shit.He definitely has gaul.Gots to say that.

Scatman

Say what? [Pause] You mean that is it false? Fakery?No definite date of origin? It just appeared?

Kool Kat

Maybe he's just sayin' that jazz does not fit into the European, a European, what did you call that thing, Off Beat?

Off Beat

Aesthetics fit within a European centered definition of beauty.

[Kool Kat changes back to local speech for a moment.]

Kool Kat

Yea, dats de word I was searchin' for.Eurocentric.

Scatman

So the man is sayin' that he cannot measure our beauty through our music called jazz?

Ain't that what aesthetics mean?

Off Beat

I suppose that you can put it that way. You can put it like that.

Scatman

He must feel that something is missin' in the music. That's what makes it imperfect.

Off Beat

But it is an art as he defines it. An imperfect art to be exact.

Kool Kat

What makes jazz an imperfect art?

Off Beat

The principle that any performer of the music must improvise while performing.

Scatman

Improvise his performance.

Kool Kat

Spontaneous performance.

BQ

Can beauty be created spontaneously in music?

Kool Kat

What type of aesthetic is that?

Off Beat

A `non-aesthetic.'

Kool Kat: What that mean?

Off Beat

It means that aesthetics is a western process as he understands and applies it. That is difficult when you try to apply western aesthetics to a post western art. To a universal art with expansive dimensions.

BQ

HO! HO! Aren't we getting mighty wordy--here?

Off Beat

His principle works well with European Classic music. Its critics have made all music art subject to its definition of music, however.

Round `Bout

But they ought to. They are learned intellectuals who invented themselves to study European artistic culture of a certain happening. The principle must be completely modified to explain what is going on in jazz a musician's music.

Scatman

That makes jazz an accidental creation. Its compositions are therefore accidental when at their best.

Off Beat

Oh, I agree with that.

[The congas of Jim Riley, a.k.a. Jumo Santos, can be heard clearly in this movement of Bitches Brew. By now, all of the shop is grooving to the magnetic force of the African drums and other percussions. A funky groove is now brewing. Critics and all are moving to the music of Miles Davis as though they have no care in the world.]

{Everybody's involvement in the music allows Off Beat to rethink his notion of jazz, the imperfect art.}

Off Beat

Of course, [Bringing everybody back to the discussion.] it was an accident of history but that accident had a historical movement in which its investors directly participated. It could never have happened otherwise. The cultural elite is bankrupt. That is why they pay so much for creativity. No matter how much material wealth they possess, they cannot create an original music such as jazz. They can own its copyright but they cannot produce it. Their ownership is false. They do not own the composition, only the rights to reproduce or hide its memory. Although they may buy rights to there aesthetics imperfections, they are frauds because they claim ownership to what they can never own. That is the privilege of the most favored. They become immortal through what ever creativemaster pieces they can buy of a dead immortal. The immortals abstractions make the most favored, the cultural elite, immortal through the purchase of the collections of immortal works.

Scatman

Spoken like a true Marxist of criticism.Historical circumstances always favor the least favored to invent the impossible.

Kool Kat

What ever you'd like to say, jazz could not have beeninvented by the white elite. Or, black elite for dat matter.

[Off Beat responds to a cheap swipe at his analysis.]

Off Beat

I do not care what Marx said. If he said it too, cool.That means he might be just about as bright as I am. No problem.

Scatman

Yea, jazz could have only come out of the black experience.maybe some other music might have evolved, but it didn't.The question is moot as far as I am concerned.

Kool Kat

I `on't Know. I don't know `bout dat.Them cats out in the territory and up in the east wouldn't exactly sittin' on their asses, you know.Alright.Gimme some. [Slap five.] {Now on a roll.}Why they always try to take what we gots?Ain't never satisfied. Greedy muthas.

Round `Bout

Avarice.

Scatman

You wanna know what the real problem is?

BQ: {Singing}

That seems to be what we're talking about.

Scatman

Oh, smart shit now.[Everybody laughs] We talkin' about direct exposure.

Kool Kat

What you mean, Scatman?

Scatman

You know.In the commercials, soundtracks.But people don't know it's jazz they are listening to.They think it's pop.

Kool Kat

Pop as in soda water.

BQ {Singing}

Yo, man be serious.

Scatman

Cain't carry on no serious conversation without some damn interruption.

Kool Kat

AH! Man, I'm sorry.I was only havin' some fun.Lightin' up.You muthas tak this shit too serious.Ain't nothin' but a game.White-tees game.

Off Beat

This is serious.

BQ {Singing}

Yo man.Get back to the point.

Off Beat

The circumstances that allowed jazz to be discovered are unique.They had to be to create the music the way they did.

Scatman

I don't buy that New Orleans bull, New Orleans wasn't the only place jazz was evolvin.'

Off Beat

You said that before.We heard you, but the fact of the matter is hip hop was started in the Bronx.Not Jamaica. Not North Carolina.Not Brooklyn, but the Bronx. The circumstances and creative energy were ripened together.Bebop was refined on the road and in the Harlem. Brooklyn and Newark clubs.New Orleans and Galveston gave us impressions of what it might look like in its early stages.Chi Town, Kansas City, Oklahoma City, St. Louis, Memphis, Dallas, Houston and San Antonio gave us a chance to refine and blues it up some more.I am sure that there were places like

Tulsa, Baltimore, New York City, Los Angeles, etcetera, doing their thing with music. But it didn't materialize in those places the way we know it today. The key word is materialize. I am certain that there were musicians in other towns who were moving in the direction New Orleans music finally hit, that accounts for its beautiful blue-sey sound coming out of the Southwest, but New Orleans opened the door to this great music.

Kool Kat

Are you saying that jazz would not have developed elsewhere? That the door would not have opened otherwise?

Off Beat

Why do you do that to me Kool? I just answered your question with the names of Tulsa, Memphis, Dallas, etcetera to make that same point, and you ask me the question that I just answered. But, to answer your question, yes I do believe that black creative music would have materialized elsewhere. That was bound to happen. I do not know that it would be called jazz, however. Jazz you up means to have sex with you.

BQ {Singing}

And we been using it all the time. Jazz, Jazz, Jazz. I gonna jazz you, I gonna jazz you, I gonna jazz you up with my jazz, jazz, jazz.

Off Beat

Black music was the blues in irregular time. The music we call jazz assumed the role of expanding it in as many ways as it could. The question would be, do we have to call it jazz for the music to have done that?

Scatman

As quite as it is kept, the blues is really the basis for the development of jazz as we know it today. World music. Reggae. Rock 'n Rhythm. Hillbilly country. Afro-pop, ad infinitum. All you needed was three tones.

Kool Kat

What about improvisation?

Scatman

Louis Armstrong.

Kool Kat

I don't understand how Gioia should say this was a historical accident. All of the right ingredients were there. That was no accident.

Scatman

Louis Armstrong. The least favored of the least favored. That could only be a historic accident, historical accident. Which one?

BQ {Singing}

Bias. Bias permits those from the most favored to claim superiority with out demonstrating such claims.

BQ Tenor {Singing}

That is because they can buy what others create and call it their own.

BQ {Singing}

Is this how it becomes high art?

Off Beat

So it seems. Thus, blues is country folk, rhythm `n blues is urban common folk and jazz is a pop art sort of. Almost high art.

Scatman

The problem with high art is the musician is divorced from the music. The composition is examined like a mathematical problem.

Off Beat

That approach creates a problem for jazz doesn't it?

Kool Kat

Sho' does. How can a cat listen to Hank Mobley or Junior Cook with the Horace Silver Quintet or Sextet and divorce them from what they are doin'? The sound they are creating is the medium. There is no score apart from that sound for them for that moment. The sound they create for that moment iswhat's happenin.' That's the joint.

Off Beat

Gunther Schuller did it.

Kool Kat

Did what?

Off Beat

He took score and transcribed it. He's a musician- musicologist who developed an intellectual affection for jazz.

On Looker

Andrew White transcribed `Trane. John Coltrane. So did Odean Pope of Phili.

[Nobody hears/listens to On Looker's always timely and brilliant comments.]

Scatman

When you say jazzz you mean the music or the musician?

Off Beat

Musicology is a very defined field.

{Still Referring to Andrew White}

On Looker

Would you call him a musicologist?

{Again On Looker is ignored by everyone. Not intentionally, they just do not have him in their consciousness. They are not listening to the Looker On.}

Scatman

Like economics.

Kool Kat

How do you mean?

Scatman

Economists study the market forces as some statistical phenomenon.

Kool Kat

Rather than as people.

Scatman

Yes. You must look at the product, at the commodity. The outcome not the personality who made it. The product becomes the commodity, the personality is simply a tool, a vehicle.

Kool Kat

The product takes on a life of its own apart from the creator. It that what you mean?

Scatman

Yea, I suppose.

Kool Kat

Usin' that analogy, what do the notes tell you about the music?

Scatman

How the composition develops.

Kool Kat

And, that's suppose to tell you what about the musician?

Scatman

How the composer was thinking. What ws going on musically.

Kool Kat

But with jazz you have to see the musician to really learn what is happenin.' All musicians know that.

Scatman

Does that make jazz musicians musicologists?

Kool Kat

How do you mean?

Scatman

All the cats I know listen to and see as many musicians they can. They actually want to see the performers execute that sound and improvisation in person.

Kool Kat

Ain't that a study of execution and technique?

Scatman

They study the composition, too.The music being played.It's just for creative musicians, they combine the two.I don't know of a musician who does not try to see all of the masters no matter the instrument.

Kool Kat

Is that because of the oral tradition black musicians bring to creative music?To their creative labor?

Off Beat

I suppose.Listening is not a natural outgrowth of an oral tradition.

Scatman

How do you mean?

Off Beat

Listening, especially to creative music requires consciousness.You have to consciously hear what is being played.Consciously hear what you are listening to.Consciously listen to what you hear. It is training.Practice. Continuously.

Kool Kat

To learn, you mean?

Off Beat

To learn.To appreciate.To understand it's aesthetic principle.It does operate according to its own aesthetic principle you know.

Scatman

How do you mean?

Off Beat

For creative music out of the African American experience to function according to that cultural tradition, it must practice the rules of that tradition.The aesthetic rules of African American approach to the arts in general and to music in particular must be observed.

Kool Kat

But how do we learn those rules?The rules?

Off Beat

By listening and practice.Jazz must be listened to actively.It must be explored in terms of texture, sound, space, time, rhythm, on and on.The music is at its best when the musician is able to combine all of those elements into a masterpiece.

BQ {Singing}

Like Black Saint and Sinner.Charles Mingus is who did it.

Kool Kat

Who was dat?Mingus?Yea, that was genius.I mean genius.Call it genuis.Call it Mingus.

Scatman

HA! HA! HA! AH! HA! You turn the record over and it reverses the composition.HA! HA!

He plays it backward. HA! HA! Backward is forward is backward.

Off Beat

I always thought that was so funny.So original.

Scatman

Only Mingus could do that.

Off Beat

But again it was through listening and practice.

Scatman

I don't mean that it was unimportant, but for Mingus it had to be more than that. More than listening and practice.

Off Beat

Oh, and that's not all.He had to develop a technique that would allow him to compose with the ear of a bass player.

Kool Kat

Well, he used the piano.

Scatman

As a bassist. There was nothin' wrong with it. Matter of fact, his unique ear allowed him to compose in a very original way.

Kool Kat

Yea, he nearly starved to death.

Scatman

He lost contact with reality for the same reason Bird shot dope.

Kool Kat

What was that?

BQ {Singing}

RACISM. RACISM. RACISM.

Off Beat

Mingus could not deal with the racism he saw, felt too well.

BQ {Singing}

Too well. He knew it too well. Racism was his nemesis that he knew too well.

Off Beat

It kills those before their time who see too much. The bebop musicians saw what the others had seem but they were less inclined to compromise with it. They were not going to compromise with racism. Racism made no sense to these geniuses.

BQ {Singing}

Sick. Racism is sick. It is only a trick. Racism is a trick, but it sure is sick. Racism is sick.

Kool Kat

Mean! Lightnin' Hopkins said that the whiteman was real mean. For no reason that he could ever figure out.

Off Beat

That meanness had a purpose.

96

Kool Kat

What?

Off Beat

Exploitation. The windfall that comes to the music industry is the surplus from thecreative labor of jazz musicians. It is through their labor that the returns to the music business are so high.

Scatman

Yea, they should at least qualify for the funding the museums qualify for.

Round `Bout

I agree, there should be a budget item that deals with culture. The arts and music should be supported as national treasures. Especially American originated music such as jazz. All creative music should receive funding as a cultural investment.

Off Beat

Now that is an excellent idea. The only problem is the grants will go to those who do not really create the music because they can right the proposals. And, have the credentials.

Kool Kat

{Again showing his language skills.}They would have one argue that they, as the most qualified scholars, are who should study the music. Musicians are then given minimum sums by these scholars because the amount granted are so small that it may be cheaper to do it yourself without any funding.

BQ {Singing}

They would successfully argue their case of superiority. They would show theirbrains. Their credentials! Their fame!

Kool Kat

Even though they have not added any value to the world's art music with a popular ring, with a popular appeal.

Scatman

You see, the Americans want to have an American culture without investing in its indigenous music. They really are only beginning to think of it as their music.

Off Beat

Much of that has to do with how culture is practiced and promoted.If the emphasis is on white sex young blood middle class style few get to see or hear other more interesting aspects of this culture.

Scatman

HA! HA! AH! AH! HA! The music in the background is jazz presented as a commercial soundtrack.

Kool Kat

While is sex selling what ever product sex is needed to sell.

BQ {Singing}

I'm gonna sex you up. I gonna jazz you up.I gonna sex you up.

BQ Tenor {Singing}

Why is the aesthetics value of jazz lost?

Off Beat

It seems to be.The aesthetics go unappreciated. The music is appreciated for its appeal to a consumer purchasing another product, not the music that sold you the product.

Scatman

But as a music form it has beauty in its own right.

BQ {Singing}

The messenger gets lost in the message.The producer becomes a victim of her product.

Off Beat

I say message because obviously consumers be they at Red Lobster or Chili's find the music appealing.They simplydo not know how to relate to this music.They do not know the names of the artists most often.Somehow the consumer does not associate the music they hear with anyone real.The music as shopping music is somehow distant from the originators of the music.

Kool Kat

The people who play it every night.It's like no one cares about the engine of a car as long as it runs.However, let the car engine break down and all hell breaks loose. [Slap five]

HA! HA! HA!

BQ {Singing}

And somebody would be ready to kick ass.HA! HA! HA!

BQ {Response}

Show 'nough.Show 'nough.HA! HA!

Kool Kat

And that's the same way they treat jazz.The beauty and the ability of this music to make any people move if they would only listen is honored by employing jazz riffs as commercials.

BQ {Singing}

The music makes you wanna...

Scatman

But the musicians are paid too little to claim that the rewards these commercials and shopping music bring in are in any way beneficial to them.

Off Beat

The aesthetics of Black Music is never considered important enough to receive commercial support by the record companies of the U.S.Today others receive royalties for music compositions they in no way created or contributed to.

Scatman

To use what Daniel Patrick Monahan said,jazz suffers from `benign neglect.'[Slap five]

Off Beat

Max got the, uh! what's the name of that prize Max Roach got?

{Without answering,...}

Scatman

That should be his salary annually, at least. How much was it?

99

Kool Kat

I think it was three or four hundred thousand dollars.

Scatman

That should be his salary at some university in the east.

Round `Bout

You know, he a college professor at one of them big universities out east. What's its name?

Off Beat

U. Mass?

BQ {Singing}

U MASS, you know, the University of Massachusetts. He been there at least twenty-five years.

BQ {Singing}

Make sure you tell then it is in Amherst, not Boston. Make sure it is Amherst.

Kool Kat

The music is awarded all of these meaningless titles that carry no prize money. It's like `musicians are use to livin' poor.'

BQ {Singing}

Anybody else who plays music for a living is a fool.

BQ{Response}

More like Michael Jordan than Michael Jackson.

Kool Kat

Ain't no money unless you sign with a good pop group that pay well.

Scatman

But then your creativity suffers.

Kool Kat

Something has to give my man.Can't have it all.

BQ {Singing}

Prince has it all.

BQ {Response}

No he does not, it is Warner Brothers.They possess his name.In the name is the basis of the claim.

Kool Kat

Yea, but you ain't no prince.Besides Prince is a pop star.Prince ain't no Monk, either.

{Silence}

Round `Bout And, Prince is not Prince any more.

{Simultaneously}

Kool Kat

How so?What is he?

Scatman

How come?Who is he?

Round 'Bout

He's one who said if I cannot use my name I will name myself whereby you must call me Prince anyway.He gave himself one of those Egyptian Hieroglyph names that only he seems to be able to say.So everyone says, `formally kmown as Prince.'

Kool Kat

Can you pronounce it.

Round `Bout

Yea, I have heard him pronounce it.

Kool Kat

Pronounce it?

Round `Bout

I can't.I hear him call his name, but I do not know what he said after he says it.

Pro

YO!Cut the name calling.The point is unless you can sell yourself you won't sell your product.That's the bottom line.

BQ {Singing}

That is the bottom line.That is the bottom line.

Scatman

Damn dat imperfect art bull shit, we got musicians starvin.'

Kool Kat

So how does jazz the aesthetic get its people work?

Off Beat

Well, jazz exponents seem to operate according to the principle that the highest form of art is to create or invent musical ideas more or less spontaneously.The critical parallel demands that you do this with your own sound that is recognizable to everybody in the know.

BQ {Singing}

That is the ultimate.The ultimate is sound.How you sound.Let me hear your voice.Let us see if you have your own voice or is your sound borrowed.

BQ {Respondents}

What can you say?What notes can you play? Have you listened to Coltrane today?Is Miles on your CD tray?How much do you know?Are your notes just show? To show that you can play what was played yesterday?

BQ {Singing}

But that is not all. That is not all.I say that is not all.It is not all.

BQ {Respondents}

What else?What else is there?What else is there to learn about Monk?

Thelonious Monk? What else must we learn?From Monk.

102

Off Beat

What was that a Ballad for An Imperfect Art you were giving us there? Controlled spontaneity.Coloring.Rhythm.It can go on forever.It has become a very studied art.

The jazz musician does everything with the music he hears.

Kool Kat

You mean, they suppose to.They don't very often, now, but they suppose to.Jazz has lost something.

Off Beat

That spontaneity must continue to grow, expand.A creative musician's labor is never at rest while in performance.That requires hard work.Very hard work.

Kool Kat

What are you talking about?

Off Beat

The musician is at rest when she knows that she can convert those haunting ghosts of the middle passage into passion sounds that strike the soul of its listeners with the beauty, pain, torment, love, struggle, survival, progression...

Kool Kat

...Yea, okay man.We get the point.We see where you are going with that.

Round `Bout: The musician is at rest if he knows how to ward off those haunting ghosts that Feeds this energy,this passion if you will.

Off Beat

So Monk, Thelonious Monk, act as a spiritual force that feed this energy, passion of sound.

Pro

If they don't ward off those ghosts, they often find themselves resorting to drugs like heroin and cocaine.Or, Alcohol.

Scatman

Exactly!The music is too demanding in its highest aesthetic aim.

BQ{Singing}

Say what?What did I hear you say?

Off Bear

The Question is, is the aim too high?Can the aim be accomplished?

Pro

By this generation.Others past have already done so.This group seems to be caught up in a lost time warp.I wish them well.They must begin to experiment.Do not accept the orthodoxy that is ruling today.The mainstream is one of many streams that flow into jazz, the global village music.

Off Beat

The music places such a demand on the abilities of the performer.Whether it is through spontaneous improvisation or a scored composition the goal is the same.

Kool Kat

What's that?

Off Beat

A masterpiece right there on the spot.

Scatman

And, gone as soon as it is invented.

Kool Kat

That requires lots of stamina.

Off Beat

And spirit.Creative energy does not work in the direction of aesthetics attainment for a jazz worker unless there is some kind of spiritual oneness present.

Kool Kat

The emotion too.

Scatman

Yes, emotion plus.Feeling.Feeling should always be present.Good, bad, it don't matter as long as feeling is there.

Kool Kat

Not all musicians can feel that emotion. They all can't play with emotion every night.

Off Beat

I am sure that there are musicians who do not put their hearts and soul into their music.

However, when you perform jazz if the feeling is not there, everyone in the place knows it.

As an example, during the period of the 1980's you might have heard that quite frequently.

Kool Kat

Yea, that is when I am...

Scatman

Oh man, back then things were bad. Times were hard. That cat might not have eaten that day. Anything might have happened that day.

Kool Kat

How you mean?

Off Beat

Remember during the eighties we went through the worse depression since the late nineteen forties. It was rough on night clubs and musicians then. No gigs. No rehearsal time. No practice. If you didn't know the tune you might not get the next gig. You came in prepared rehearsal or not.

Kool Kat

You are sayin' that the economic conditions affected how the music sounded.

Scatman

You gots it.

Kool Kat

Money!

Scatman

I couldn't have said it better.

Kool Kat

What about the aesthetics?I thought you said the question raised was around aesthetics.

How one performs on the chosen instrument is measured by what the piece accomplishes aesthetically. Is that not the thing we were talking about?

Scatman

What is the question?

Off Beat

The question is, does jazz aesthetically transcend value judgment?How does creative music qualify as a non-aesthetic process?

Scatman

HA! I get it.If jazz operates outside the European cultural dynamic it cannot be fairly judged by that aesthetic.Heavy!

Kool Kat

Give it here baby. [Extends hand to Off Beat, Scatman being in between thinks that the hand extension is for him, so Kool Kat ends up slapping both hands almost simultaneously,]

{Slap Five}

[The place breaks up laughing over how Kool Kat recovers when he sees a potential disaster and turns it into a well choreographed slap five.]

Kool Kat

The question is, however, does it transcend any aesthetics' ability to judge it?

Off Beat

Or, has it created its own?

Kool Kat

Aesthetics?

Scatman

Exactly. Tradition. I would say aesthetic tradition.

Off Beat

I have no problem with that. No problem. Because that standard has been set. The issue facing jazz musicians is racism. That other thing only serves as a cover-up.

Kool Kat

A facade.

Scatman

The real issue when you come down to it is racism. All of the rest are support casts.

Bottom line.

BQ   {Singing}

Bottom line. Bottom line. Bottom line.

BQ {Respondents}

A facade is a fraud. A fraud, a facade.

Off Beat

I call it the least favored position. The jazz worker occupies the least favored position in the market place. Returns on investment tend to be disproportionately below what is made from their creative labor by other market players.

Round`Bout

To understand a music you must understand the cultural context in which it operates and develops. A music that continues to reproduce itself obviously originates within a very rich dynamic with its own aesthetics. The base of jazz is African American experience, its culture. Scholars must study and appreciate that culture if they are in any way goingto understand the value derived from its music. To the degree you understand the culture you will appreciate its music.

Kool Kat

You are saying that you cannot enjoy jazz unless you understand it.

Off Beat

No! Anyone can enjoy any music that pleases them.

Kool Kat

Then what do you mean?

Round`Bout

I was referring to scholars who use their own cultural reference points to explain other people's cultures.Other people's art.Other people's music.How othe people live. No two cultures are exactly alike even when they speak the same language.When other factors enter the picture cultures can differ greatly.

On Looker

What is culture?

Round `Bout

A culture embodies the doings and beliefs of a people.

Scatman

Say man, you're gettin' too complex for my man here.

Kool Kat

No he isn't.

Scatman

`scuse me.[Slap Five] {Everybody laughs at Scatman.]

Kool Kat

My motto is if you ain't from it, you ain't of it.

Scatman

Jingoist.

Round` Bout

Anyway scholars must respect the value of any culture they plan to investigate, no matter what aspect they choose to examine.A lack of respect will certainly not contribute to understanding correctly what they might attempt to explain.

Scatman

So what are you saying?Does jazz have an aesthetic base?Or, are its imperfections a hindrance to it having one?

Off Beat

On the contrary, it is imperfection that makes jazz a creative art.Creativity is placed in its most challenging position with jazz.It's the improvisation combined with sound/style that offers the true test to the creative musician.

BQ {Singing}

What do you have to say with your musical instrument?Do you have a voice that I can recognize?

BQ {Respondents}

You sound like someone else I recognize. You did not practice to win the prize.Whose that sound you're playing there.A Kopy Kat like you will go no where.No where in jazz.

Off Beat

You see,creativity is an art.Creative music that revolves around improvisation lives or dies by that art, not by how someone evaluates the musical form it assumes at a particular time in its evolution.So, if jazz lives or dies, it will not be because of how some critics review its players.Further, the aesthetics of jazz will continue to operate as the objective test of the beauty this music creates as long as the musician operates by the rules of performance this music has established.

BQ {Singing}

Right on!! Right on! [Everybody slap high five in a way of over weight men.]

Off Beat

To understand the music's aesthetics one must understand the feelings this culture possess, and how these feelings are expressed in the many varied musical forms and genres we seem to never tire of reconstructing.

Scatman

That ought to be it. [Everybody slap five celebrating their `bull shit' talk.Good bull shit talk.] HA! HA! HA!

On Looker

Gentlemen, we have just heard a critique of Ted Gioia's "The Imperfect Art: Reflection on Jazz and Modern Culture."Cool.

Bitches Brew by the Miles Davis Band is winding down with Miles Runs The VOO DOO Down.In walks Crazy Man the comedian. Right on queue, he walks in to lighten the atmosphere after that heavy discussion about that thing, music, that James Harris calls an imperfect art.

Root Doctor
Hoo Doo Man
(a play about Robert Johnson)

Delridge La Veon Hunter
(Read Aloud)

Blues is
Poetic
Therapeutic
Prognosticator
En-gung
Griot equivalent
New
Old
Simple
Ambiguous
Complex
Different
With that
Peculiar
Sad sound
As a reframe
A pain
Inside
Hurts
Just
As
Much

Characters

Hoo Doo Man

Root Doctor

{Root Doctor is a woman while Hoo Doo Man is self-explanatory!}

[Should be read aloud.] {Strong Southern Ebonics}

Blues for Robert Johnson

[Singing Blues]

Hoo Doo Man

I gots a woman who'll tak me when I ain't gots no where to go.

I say, I gots me a woman who'll tak me in, but I ain't gots no where to go.

That'sthe life of a rolling stone, ain't never lived no place I ever seen befo'. Gots a woman who'll tak me in when I ain't gots no where else to go.

I say, gots me a woman who'll tak me in, but I gots some place else to go.

Reframe: That's the life of a rollin' stone, ain't never been no place I ever been befo'.

Chorus

Gotta gal, gotta gal that I love. Gotta gal, gotta gal, gotta gal that I love. I love dat woman 'cause she so sweet to me.

Root Doctor

I see that you're fan of Robert Johnson. That was Robert Johnson's tune you were singing just now, wasn't it? I always know his music when I hear it. Interesting character Robert Johnson. Very interesting character, and the best blues singer, too.

Hoo Doo Man

Well no, it was not by him as much as it was 'bout Robert Johnson,so they say.

Root Doctor

OH! It sounded just like something he might do.

Hoo Doo Man

That was my intent.

Root Doctor

What do you mean?

Hoo Doo Man

You know, Robert Johnson died a very tragic death. The song sort 'ogives a frame work for explaining the tragedy.

111

Root Doctor

How do you mean?

Hoo Doo Man

Robert was a Hoo Doo man. He believed.

Root Doctor

He was a ladies man, wasn't he?

Hoo Doo Man

Ever where he went, he always had somebody there to take care of him.

Root Doctor

A rolling stone.

Hoo Doo Man

Okay, that might be what you can call him, but I always think of Robert Johnson as a ladies man.

Root Doctor

A womanizer according to some.

Hoo Doo Man

Okay, if you want to thank so, I accept that.

Root Doctor

Now, the tragedy? I heard that he got shot or stabbed in some little town in Alabama for messing with some dude's ole' lady.

Hoo Doo Man

Poison.

Root Doctor

I beg you pardon?

Hoo Doo Man

Poison. P-O-I-S-O-N! It was poison that sent him to his maker. And, it was Mississippi. Greenwood. Three forks. 1938. He died August 16. Three days it took. Long and slow. No mercy. Lawd! Lawd!

Root Doctor

POISON? POISON! Dawn! Poison! Who gave it to him? I bet it was it was a woman. Cain't put nothin' past a woman. A woman did it. How'd she do it? When she do it? When he was eating some food? HA!HA!HA!HA! The man done gon' down to Mississippi and let a jealous country woman do him in.

112

Hoo Doo Man

HA! You see. All you can think of is men shooting men and men cutting men and women feeding some unsuspecting damn fool man poison. It was poison, but I didn't say it was a woman. It was a man.

Root Doctor

A man? A man murdered Robert Johnson with poison? HA!HA!HA!AH!HA!HA!Is you serious? Tell me more. How did it happen? How'd he do it?

Hoo Doo Man

Well, you know, dudes back then were players, 'specially if they were musicians. I know, my uncle was one.

Root Doctor

And handsome.

Hoo Doo Man

How did you know? Of course.

Root Doctor

What did he do?

Hoo Doo Man: Apparently, he messed with the wrong dude's wife.

Root Doctor

And, it cost him.

Hoo Doo Man

It cost him his life.

Root Doctor

So come on, now. You still ain't tell me what happen. Poison is serious. That sounds like that Hoo Doo shit. You know what I mean?

Hoo Doo Man

I know what you mean.

Root Doctor

So, what happen? Who did it?

Hoo Doo Man

Well ain't nobody charged. But, from what I gather, sounds like the barman set him up.

Root Doctor

Bartender? A bartender> What the bartender...?

Hoo Doo Man

He had the best motive.

Root Doctor

So, he gave him the drank?

Hoo Doo Man

No, not exactly.

Root Doctor

Then how he do it? In the food. He ate some bar-be-que at the jook house he was playing at. That's right ain't it? Well. Say something?

Hoo Doo Man

I am if you let me. No food was eaten that was poison. It was in a bottle he drank out of.

Root Doctor:

I told you he put it in his drank, why didn't you say so?

Hoo Doo Man

I said no to your comment that it was the bartender who gave him the drink. I told you no one was charged.

Root Doctor Why not?

Hoo Doo Man

The bartender did not give him the bottle.

Root Doctor

Who did?

Hoo Doo Man

Somebody else?

Root Doctor

Who was he?

Hoo Doo Man

Nobody knows. Probably a kind of conspiracy in that the bartender gave someone at the bar and told him to give Bob a drink on the house.

Root Doctor

And, nobody saw it.

Hoo Doo Man

Come on, this kat was crazy. He had to be.

Root Doctor

How do you mean?

Hoo Doo Man

You gone tak' a gig at a joint owned by the man whose wife you gone/done hit on while you on stage, I'd say you crazy. She just sat there and enjoyed it.

Root Doctor

He must have did it. Damn! She was? That's about a crazy mutha', huh? I didn't know that he was that gone. You know I heard some stuff, but I didn't know that he went that far. So how'd they give it to 'em?

Hoo Doo Man

Somebody walked up and gave it to him.

Root Doctor

And, he took it?

Hoo Doo Man

Oh, Robert would try anything. Whiskey made him act like the devil.HA! HA! HA! HA!

Root Doctor

So they walked up to him and gave it to him.

Hoo Doo Man

Yep!

Root Doctor

And, he drunk it?

Hoo Doo Man

NAW!

Root Doctor

NAW? He didn't? But, I thought you said he did?

Hoo Doo Man

Let me tell this story. He didn't at first 'cause his friend Sonny Boy Williamson was playing there at the time. He knocked it out of Robert's hand. When he did, when he took the bottle, he told Robert "don't never tak' no bottle from nobody that's open, with the seal broke, you don't know what might be in it."

Root Doctor

What did Robert say? "Yea, man thanks, forgot 'bout that. Phew?" Huh, what he say?

Hoo Doo Man

HA! Not Robert, he was stuck on his self. He said, "man you betta not ever do that again. You better not ever knock a bottle 'o whiskey outa my han' again." Damn, what's wrong wid' you, you crazy?'

Root Doctor

Whaat? You kiddin'? Nobody's that dumb.

Hoo Doo Man

NAW? Nobody? Robert was. Stubborn, that's what he was.

Root Doctor

I wouda left the kat alone after that. Only a fool would not see that and heed a fair warning.

Hoo Doo Man

That's what happened. His musician friend, Sonny Boy Williamson, said to me, "I couldn't stand there and see him die lik that. So, I left. I felt like I was numb. That's the last time I saw him alive. Robert Johnson. That dude could compose a song. He was pretty good on the guitar, too."

Root Doctor

What happen next? He thought he was a lady's man. And, an original guitar player.

Hoo Doo Man

Yea, I know! Eventually, somebody brought over another bottle.

Root Doctor

Unsealed?

Hoo Doo Man

Yep!

Root Doctor

And he drunk it?

Hoo Doo Man

He drank it.

Root Doctor

Blues! Hootchie Chootchie Man

[John Lee Hooker sings, "I'm Bad Like Jesse James."]

John Lee Hooker

I bad, like Jesse James. UH! HUH! I had a friend one time. Least I thought I did. He come to me, say Jonnie. Say, what man? I'm out doors. I say, yea. I taken de cat in. Cet' me a place to stay, and I found out he goin' around town telling everybody that he got my wife. And, I gets mad. I goes to the cat like a good guy should. I say look man, I'm gonna warn you, just one time. Next time I warn you, I'm gon use my gun, 'cause I'm mad. I'm bad, like Jesse James. I'm mad, I'm so mad. I gonna run you dis mornin'. I got three boys do my dirty work. Now, you don't see me, I'm the big boss. I do the pay off, after, after they tak' care of you, in they own way. They may shoot you. They may cut you. They may drown you. I just don't know. I don't care. Long as de tak care of you in they own way. I'm so mad. I'm bad this mornin'. Like Jesse James. They gonna tak you right down by the riverside. Now, four is goin' down ain't but three comin' back. I'm bad. Like Jesse James. They don tie yo hand. They gonna tie your feet. They gonna gag your throat, where you cain't hide now non'. Cryin' won't help you non'. The gonna set you in the water, where bubbles comin' up. OH! DRRRRRRRRRRRRR!

Hoo Doo Man

Yea, the real blues. The Hootchie Chootchie Man. John Lee Hooker said, 'the blues was here when the world was born.' Ain't that bright? From the "Original Sin" up to now humans have had the blues.

Root Doctor

That's deep! Didn't he tell the dude, "I'll take you out?

Hoo Doo Man

Somebody like Lightnin' would say that, too. He was an original composer.

Root Doctor

Didn't he say, it'll take you out!

Hoo Doo Man

Yes, he did. But, it was Lou Rawls that talked about that tobacco road so many blues musicians walked down.

Hoo Doo Man

You are using that, as a metaphor, 'cause Robert ain't walked nowhere. Lightnin' did, but Robert wouldn't walk down to the grocery store to get a pack of cigarettes.

Root Doctor

Probably smoked Chesterfields or Camels.

Hoo Doo Man

Or, Pall Mall, maybe Lucky Strike. What? Robert ain't gon' walk nobody's mile. Robert never confused himself with a camel. HA! HA! HA!

Root Doctor

HA! HA! HA! But Lightnin' didn't care. He just wanted to make tracks.

Hoo Doo Man

Interesting. I suppose that explains a major difference in their approaches to blues

Root Doctor

And music.

Hoo Doo Man

Yea, you're right. The only thing they seem to have in common is...

Root Doctor

...Both were tremendous in their renditions of blues.

Hoo Doo Man

I was thinking more about their country background. They both are good country musicians.

Root Doctor

That's true. How easily we forget.

Hoo Doo Man

What's that?

Root Doctor

The country in 'country and western' came from the country music sung by the black farmers, tenant farmer, and sharecropper when they sat down all day Saturday at the cotton gin waiting their turn to turn in their bails and get their pay, if there was any.

Hoo Doo Man

That's true. I remember this old man who always had his guitar. He would play alone.

Root Doctor

And, another kat has a harp. He'd sit all day and play his harmonica. He had this real piercing sound. One that would not go away!

Hoo Doo Man

Sure did. Somebody always had a harmonica that wailed.

Root Doctor

…and, Kazoo.

Hoo Doo Man

And, Jews harp.

Root Doctor

They could play. HA! HA! HA! HA!

Hoo Doo Man

Country music at its best. But, my interest is in the differences between Robert and Lightnin' Hopkins approach to music.

Root Doctor

Well, Lightnin' s music was very eclectic and improvisational. He could sing about, about any subject on the spot. His facility for song creation was tremendous.

Hoo Doo Man

And Robert?

Root Doctor

Robert composed these interesting mystical surreal songs. You know like, 'Kind hearted Woman Blues.' You know, a lot of Hoo Doo stuff like, 'I'll Dust My Broom."

Hoo Doo Man

Lightnin' sang a lot of social commentary.

Root Doctor

Robert didn't sing as many—nobody did for that matter—but the few he did…Phew!

Hoo Doo Man

Like what?

Root Doctor

Well, there's 'Sweet Home Chicago.'

Hoo Doo Man

That 's just a regular blues.

Root Doctor

NAW! Ain't nobody back then sang no regular blues? "Back to the Land of California, to my sweet home Chicago." Everybody knows that California was considered paradise in the days of Robert Johnson. Especially, if lived down south. And, Chicago was always home sweet home for people from Arkansas and Mississippi.

Hoo Doo Doctor

But that was to subtle to call social commentary. Lightnin' sang about slavery. You remember that tune, '1000 years my people was a slave,' when I was born they teach me this way. Tip you hat to this way. Tip you say.' Now, that's powerful stuff. No subtleties.

Root Doctor

All of Robert's music was blues commentary. But, he was more of a town crier.

Hoo Doo Man

The town crier. That's different.

Root Doctor

You know! He sang about local feelings of loneliness. Personal relations. His was the ultimate metaphor. A continuation of African Root Music. He kept Hoo Doo alive.

Hoo Doo Man

Hoo Doo a consummate African American metaphor. But, Lightnin' was one in a hundred million. One of a kind.

Root Doctor

Robert expected to die a young man. He wanted to expose his genius before he did. He did.

Hoo Doo Man

And, Lightnin' lived as though Dowling Street was the center of the universe, sit there in his chair up against the house dinking his bottle of Lone Star beer, smoking his cigarillo, and the world would pass his way.

Root Doctor

Apparently he was right.

Hoo Doo Man

But the both became immortals. Following different routes.

Root Doctor

So, what were their differences?

Hoo Doo Man

My personal opinion is Robert Johnson created a school of blues that qualifies as the "Julliard" of entrepreneurial music {no pun intended]. No other genre or class of music has sold as many copies of recordings of musicians who came from the Robert Johnson Conservatory of Music, to my knowledge. Yet, he would hardly qualify for the 'major composer' category of the New York Public Library Desk Reference.

Root Doctor

HA! HA! The Duke don't qualify either for that matter.

Hoo Doo Man

I hear yea. [slap five]

Root Doctor

Heavy! And, Lightnin'?

Hoo Doo Man

Lightnin' should qualify too. On numbers alone. Lightnin'? Lightnin' there is only one Lightnin'. He is like Art Tatum in Jazz. When they cut the mold, somebody must have said…

Root Doctor

:…That's it. No more! He's the only one of that mold. I use to watch this dude over in 5th ward at the Club Matinee. The ladies would be working their tricks while Lightnin' might be giving us a commentary on sharecropping in East Texas, the Queen of England, hitch hiking, the President of the United States and any other topic someone in the group from Prairie View threw out there for critique. Man we would be sitting there watching Lightnin' play his guitar. Man, we would be sitting there watching Lightnin' play his guitar. Man, …

Hoo Doo Man

How was it?

Root Doctor

By the piece. HA! HA!

Hoo Doo Man

HA! HA! HA! HA! HA! Man, that's sexist. Where was this?

Root Doctor

In Houston, 5th Ward. On Fridays. When he was in town. Lightnin' was becoming popular again. Naw! Naw! That's the way it was. It was a free market live and let everybody work philosophy.

Hoo Doo Man

When was this?

Root Doctor

Early 1960's C.E . Things was hot musically. The music in the Long Star state was very rich at the time. Houston, Dallas, San Antonio, Temple, Bryan, Cameron all had places where some of the best acts in music came through.

Hoo Doo Man

Austin, too.

Root Doctor

That's true.

Hoo Doo Man

I know that Texas was a blues state. However, I heard that there was not that much action for the movement. I heard that blues singers did not comment on the things happening in Texas and across the south.

Root Doctor

Every state from Texas and Oklahoma to New Mexico and Arizona had movements. Often times they were before what happened in thee central south. The southwest was not behind the old south, is was ahead in most areas. As for blues singers, anyone heard of Ray Charles. But the old blues singers knew that their commentary was more like storytelling than any thing else. The reasons for the failure of blues during, if that was the case, doing the movement was the calculated effort to promote music with little substance in 'Dance with me Henry'. Odetta, who we saw in Austin, sang commentary and they called it folk. Folk music is what they called it but she, like ODETTA, sang blues. So As did Liightnin' and Leadbelly and Blind Lemon Jefferson. All of it was commentary.

Hoo Doo Man

And, don't forget Nina Simone.

[Nina Simone's "I love your Porgy" came be heard in the back ground.

Root Doctor

Oh, Yes. She was the symbolic spirit of the movement. I don't mean the 'official we shall overcome movement'. I am referring to the mood of all black college students at the time. Her record, 'I love you Porgy' played at every black college campus I knew all day every day.

[Nina stops]

Hoo Doo Man

What about Odetta? I thought she was the movement's spiritual voice.

[Odetta sings}

Root Doctor

She was the voice to the European American and urban coeds, but Nina was the voice of the "Civil Rights Movement." The Movement!

Hoo Doo Man

But that wasn't a movement song.

Root Doctor

Sure it was. It was classic. It was her voicing and the spiritual energy she fed us. Her piano playing was so free and powerful. So powerful were the two. It reflected the mood. She became the spokesperson.

Hoo Doo Man

How was that?

Root Doctor

She expressed the emotions we were feeling. She could mesmerize the audience. Like Robert did the women. I rate her with Nat 'King' Cole as a Jazz pianist. The power was in the sound.

Hoo Doo Man

BLACK POWER!

Root Doctor

BLACK POWER! BLUES POWER!

Hoo Doo Man

How did blues get such a bad rap?

Root Doctor

Elvis Presley. Ignorance, fear, real hatred for black people. Blues is 'timeless' according to Phil Wiggins. It has always bee around. It will always be around.

Hoo Doo Man

As a song!

Root Doctor

Yes, longer than scholars claim. Look at Hip Hop.

Hoo Doo Man

How so?

Root Doctor

You know the strict chronology approach to Jazz History makes everything discussed fit into a very defined way of looking at the world. One strait line. Mono! So, for them, blues began sometime between the end of our War of Liberation, the so-called Civil War, and the 1900's C.E. They disagree on the particulars, but most scholars agree on the time frame. Unbelievable!

Hoo Doo Man

I didn't know that. I did not know that scholars did not know that. I thought everybody knew that blues is as old as time. I mean, Literally it has to go back to when Africans were stolen from the old continent. At least.

Root Doctor

At least! The scholars say that Blues came out of "Spiritual and Work Songs."

Hoo Doo Man

So how did the War of Liberation become the demarcation line?

Root Doctor

Convenience and laziness. It does not upset other 'paradigms' on black music.

Hoo Doo Man

The what?

Root Doctor

The notions that 'spirituals' are the bases of African American music. That mythology comes out of the Christian paradigm. It is so western it is almost shameful.

Hoo Doo Man

Sound like Christian Doctrine is behind this scholarship. When did the music we call Spirituals began?

Root Doctor

Sometime during the turn of the 18th century! The real 'spichuls' go nearly as far back as blues. However, the Spirituals came after the Blues. These Spirituals were the Ido hymns from Nigeria. And, Blues is called "Engung" in Congo. The Angolan/Congolese brought what we call the Blues with them. That is as early as the 1600's. They were not Christians, but they had the Blues and they sang about it. The point is, Blues and Spirituals arrived here from the different streams! But, both are part of the continuum from Africa.

Hoo Doo Man

Would your repeat that, again???

[Ignoring question]   **Root ~Doctor**

124

George White of Fish University and the black college music directors who followed him unfortunately modernized the Spirituals, prematurely. They apparently felt ashamed of how the old blues/spirituals sounded to the European Americans people. These apologists felt a need to give the Spirituals some sophistication so that the most favored would not get the impression that we were a bunch of primitives.

Hoo Doo Man

How did blues get left out?

Root Doctor

Blues was Devil songs. They were not noticed as real music. The Devil songs were avoided by Christian's black and white. Only Hymns were permitted.

Hoo Doo Man

Blues was the music of fornication, blasphemy and Sin?

Root Doctor

Yes! Yes! The explanation follows the God/Lucifer thesis where god kicked Lucifer out of the Kingdom of Heaven. Blues became the music of and from Hell. Whole webs of explanations have evolved around Spirituals being the beginning of Negro slave songs.

Hoo Doo Man

How so?

Root Doctor

Group singing.

Hoo Doo Man

Okay, so?

Root Doctor

It meant that we did not know how to sing solo. That only came after the War of Liberation when the black man got his mobility, and when conditions were worse than anything he had ever seen under slavery.

Hoo Doo Man

What? Are you serious?Sharecropping was worse than slavery therefore giving blues it opportunity to be born? Are you serious?

Root Doctor

Yep! As serious as death.

Hoo Doo Man

Let me see, black people could only sing in groups?

Root Doctor

Yep, according to their thesis nobody had learned to sing solo until we met the most favored people. Negros had not figured out how to moan and groan, alone, yet.

Hoo Doo Man

A! HA! HA!AH! HAAA! HA! WHO STARTED ALL OF THAT CRAP?

Root Doctor

I heard it at the black college I attended. It came from our music teacher and choir director. He hated Jazz and its parent Blues with a passion. For him, it was not music. We were not allowed to bring the Devil Music into the music room.

Hoo Doo Man

So, what did yawl do?

Root Doctor

We took it over to the student union every Saturday. We played all day Saturday until sundown then we either went down to Houston or up to the American Woodman's Lodge in Dallas.

Hoo Doo Man

So, who started all that crap?

Root Doctor:

The list is enormous. Every scholar and critic from David Evans to Stanley Crouch.

Hoo Doo Man

Man, they obviously don't know their music cultural history or the history of the south. People would be singing Blues all the time. They didn't know what these people were singing. If they did not know, they should have researched it by reading slave narratives. The narrations were clear. The music they sang was what we call secular. The secular songs were called Devil songs during slavery. Devil songs have always meant what we call Blues today.

Root Doctor

Tell the story.

Hoo Doo Man

When a master sold a child from his or her parents, you gon' tell me ain't nobody gone sing some Blues to memorialize that happening? Huh?

Root Doctor

Not me. Carry on.

Hoo Doo Man

You gone tell me they gone get some church group together and sing "swing low sweet chariot"? That's a freedom song. "Swing Low" is an Escapist song.

RootDoctor

Most people don't know that.

Hoo Doo Man

Naw, don't tell me that bull. Somebody, I call the lyric poet is going to compose a lyric that tell the whole community about this tragic act. It ain't no group singing either. Only the lyric poet or blues singer is gone have the ability to put in words the hurt, pain, despair, hardship and terror of such deep seated hatred. Come on give me a break? You hear what I'm telling you? You hear what I'm sayin'?

Root Doctor

I hear you, Hoo Doo Man, go on with your narrative.

Hoo Doo Man

Only the Hoo Doo priest is gone have the nerve to comment musically on that matter. Blues is as natural as sadness, estrangement, and alienation. Not to sing, play-speak about it in that peculiar Blue minor tone is antithetical to black thought, to African consciousness. You hear what I'm sayin'?

Root Doctor

Keep talking! I'm listening.

Hoo Doo Man

I just find that hard to believe. The slave narratives do not support that position about there being no Blues singing during slavery.

Root Doctor

Just read the Born in Slavery narratives. There are more than enough. 2,000 thousand? So, they obviously begin with a false premise, that there is no recorded proof of this happening.

Hoo Doo Man

What about all of this oral history? We've been talking oral history for the past, whatever, however, long as we have been in these United States called America.

Root Doctor

Apparently, that don't count. They go on tellin' everybody where is the evidence, where is the proof that blues existed during slavery. They say we have records of spirituals, where are the records of blues. I tell them just look at the Devil songs.

127

Hoo Doo Man

So, Devil's music is not enough proof, huh? Well I've seen them with my own eyes, and that is proof enough for me.

Root Doctor: They go on to say, ain't no record of the people ever singin' solo.

Hoo Doo Man

And, that ain't proof enough. All of the evidence in Born in Slavery: slave narratives of the federal writers project, 1936-38 is proof enough for any body wid any sense. ·

Root Doctor

Hoo Doo Man, you are right. All of the evidence says you're right.

Hoo Doo Man

They say there ain't no photographs. Well, there ain't no need for photos with thousands of slave records of the music being performed.

Root Doctor

For the record.

Hoo Doo Man

For the record, exactly.

Root Doctor

Why would critics and scholars want to hide the evidence?

Hoo Doo Man

The slave hid blues right in front of the man 'cause the bluesman, blues woman was dangerous.

Root Doctor

Exactly. You know the lie is there was no En-gung, no Griot, priests, musicians; storytellers that came through the middle passage alive.

Hoo Doo Man

In Congo they call his music En-gung.

Root Doctor

he blues singer was militant and pulled no punches. They talked of how the master and overseer was killed by some disgruntled slaves. So, they was dangerous. They did not believe in turn the other cheek. These people came through the middle passage alive with the African stories embedded in the their cultural memories.

Hoo Doo Man

Yet, these critics want us to believe that all of that was wiped out. That we was nothing but a clean slate, that the white man destroyed every thing by the time we reach America.

Root Doctor

Or, that we were so weak that we didn't have no energy or strength to provide a challenge to the new more superior culture of whiteness.

Hoo Doo Man

Result: Everything was totally wiped out. So, according to these people, all that we have was invented here by learning the ways of the most favored, the so-called "white man."

Root Doctor

My response to all that is, what about the coachman who traveled with his "master" or "mistress" as the lover, confident, servant, slave, bodyguard, entertainer, and coachman or nanny? They did not sing nothin' but spirituals in their spare time?

Hoo Doo Man

Right on! They could sing sorrow songs or blues ballads? None carried instruments to play when they were alone? You think they sang the kind of music they performed for the master or mistress when they were alone? When the master and mistress were not around, do you think these there were ignorant niggers who did not have their own consciousness about themselves? None? Not one? No poems were blue?

Root Doctor

One thing is obvious is relation of blacks to music: it can be many or it can be one. These, musicians did not recognize any restrictions over their music. They were keepers of the culture. They were therefore invisible to the culture of whiteness. The harp players mentioned in the Christian Bible—they were black men. They were En-gung, the storytellers, the historians for a small fee of course.

Hoo Doo Man

You are saying what I'm sayin' that this music dates back to the ancients?

Root Doctor

At least. Remember John Lee Hooker and Phil Wiggins. John Lee Hooker said, that 'blues is as old as the world' while Phil Wiggins said, 'blues is timeless.'

Hoo Doo Man

I hear what you are sayin' but ain't no authority accepts what we are sayin'.

Root Doctor

I know, they do not accept our promise.

Hoo Doo Man

You might be correct about that, but where there's hurt there's the preconditions for blues.

Root Doctor

Feelings are subject to be blue and the subject matter becomes blues.

Hoo Doo Man

True! So, why such a premise among African Americans wait to be discovered by European American collectors before it would exist?

Root Doctor

You are saying that Blues did not wait for modern technology or W.C. Handy to express itself.

Hoo Doo Man

Yes, I am. As an expression, there is plenty of evidence of Blues prior to the turn of the century, before it was 'discovered' by somebody with a pen and paper to write down their discovery.

Root Doctor:

Who do you have in mind?

Hoo Doo Man

Paul Laurence Dunbar was writing it before Bessie Smith, Ma' Rainey, Memphis Minnie, Ray Charles, Diane Washington, James Brown, Charles Brown, and Robert Johnson came along.

Root Doctor

Let's take James Brown, J.B.

Hoo Doo Man

When did you first hear of James Brown? When did you first see him? Did you ever see James Brown in person?

Root Doctor

Yea, I saw him. It was when I was in college. I saw him in Houston in the Coliseum with 10,000 other black folks. That would be the 1950' early 60's.

Hoo Doo Man

When was he 'discovered' by European Americans?

Root Doctor

I don't know, the 1970's late I think. I don't remember. I don't keep up with them folks.

Hoo Doo Man

You're right. That's true.

Root Doctor

Why would we reason that Blues began so late in African American history? Or, even worse, that it is an our growth of Spirituals.

Hoo Doo Man

Wait-a-minute, it was you quoting western science as your Bible. I said…

Root Doctor

…Why would all slaves sing spirituals and "work songs" all day long, and nothin' else? I know.

Hoo Doo Man

What happened when someone's baby was kidnapped and sold to a stranger in the night? Nobody had blue feelings over that happening? Even when a wife was taken?

Root Doctor

Maybe the sang spirituals with spirit. Or, maybe they sang it blue.

Hoo Doo Man

I would think that it would be blue. I know I would. NAW! I'd be mad. Not angry, stone mad.

Root Doctor

And you sang blues songs 'bout how much sorrow you felt. Tears will not suffice.

Hoo Doo Man

It might not be me at all. It maybe somebody starts humming and moaning, and everybody would know that it was blues that was bothering him or her or the whole community.

Root Doctor

So the problem is scholars are confusing musical form with blues expression.

Hoo Doo Man

How do you mean?

Root Doctor

The old people didn't make a real distinction between Blues and Spirituals. They would sing both the same way. It was in the expression that one knew the difference. They would even use the same lyrics sometime. The important thing was feeling. You could listen and tell if they were happy or if somebody was blue.

131

Hoo Doo Man

You could hear it. Blues is blues.

Root Doctor

Blue are blues. HA! HA! HA!

Hoo Doo Man

Whatever, but that seems so logical.

Root Doctor

I know. The mistake is in the pseudo black form given to spirituals. That's European American adaptation of the original African form. If you examine the lyrics is slave songs, it's easy to see how they could be the beginning of any present day genre. There are any numbers of 'blues' songs in the slave songbooks.

Hoo Doo Man

Now that makes since.

Root Doctor

The point is, when European American scholars took note of slave songs, they were 'experts' of Black Popular Culture. In other words, one scholar might come across root music and not recognize it. We know that the most favored participated in the Hoo Doo rituals in different parts of the south; we know that they participated in New England. We also know that in New England they were burned at the stake and called 'witches of the Devil,' the most favored of the south were not as successful. In spite of every effort to totally destroy all vestiges of the African American traditional practices, they never succeeded. It's not that the south was more tolerant of the 'negroes' and there peculiar practices, they simply could not destroy them. They could not destroy Hoo Doo as the old religion.

Hoo Doo Man

No matter what they did.

Root Doctor

The 'negro' so-called is not dumb and ignorant of this move to destroy their culture. The wave of hostility was so great; all we could do was teach the basics. Even that was hard. So, operating underground protected the different vestiges of the tradition.

Hoo Doo Man

This is how they resisted cultural chauvinism. Or, should I say cultural imperialism. After all, the people enslaved were from other nations.

Root Doctor

Hoo Doo priests and Root Doctors were as deeply underground as possible. They also developed allies. They emerged as blues singers when the time was right.

Hoo Doo Man

Is that why so many blues singers could be seen after the War of Liberation, the so-called "war between-the-states?" I wondered how there were so many blues singers or lyric poets so quickly? It's like they came out of the wood works.

Root Doctor

Prohibition was over. If Phyllis Wheatley had composed militant feminist poetry would she have been published?

Hoo Doo Man

HA! HA! HA! HA! AH! AH! HA! I see what you mean.

Root Doctor

This was slavery. Why would a slave want to share their inner most thoughts with the enemy. The slave master was the enemy.

Hoo Doo Man

What about the po' whites, the other least favored people in the American Dream?

Root Doctor

What about hem?

Hoo Doo Man

They often became informed listeners of blues. They were always blue too. How do you think they got 'country?' Country was white blues.

Root Doctor:

A! I never thought of it that way. Actually I never thought of it until you mentioned it right now. I am sure that they had every reason to.

Hoo Doo Man

Why didn't they sing blues?

Root Doctor

Funny you would ask that. I had this little pamphlet- that I placed on my friend's roof and we drove off – my husband bought in the Delaware Water Gap that was written by the musicologist John Lomax at the Library of Congress. It was about the life of 'Leadbelly.' In it he mentioned that some prior research had caused him amazement.

Hoo Doo Man

What did he discover?

Root Doctor

He could not help noticing that although poor whites and poor blacks suffered the same state of oppression yet the European American poor did not sing at all. I found that rather interesting.

Hoo Doo Man

Where was this?

Root Doctor

Mississippi. Delta, I think.

Hoo Doo Man

Same conditions, exactly.

Root Doctor

The very same!

Hoo Doo Man

But they came up with country and western. That grew out of bluegrass,

Root Doctor

Country. They call it blue grass; the recording industry calls it 'country and western.' The western is an invention of Hank Williams. The country comes from blues and African songsters/musician singing to and for the most favored. They perform this music for the entertainment. Realizing that the Europeans could not sing or play instruments in all of the times, scales and rhythms the Africans brought with them, old black musicians use to play country and bluegrass-blues around Tennessee, West Virginia and Kentucky. That's how the country became attached to the western. Hank Williams was from California. That made everything from Texas to California "Country & Western"

Hoo Doo Man

When was this?

Root Doctor

On the radio you could hear during the 1930's 40's 50's.

Hoo Doo Man

Yea, about 300 years after black people arrived here on this soil.

Root Doctor

At least!

[The dialogue ends with Lightnin' Hopkins singing a blues tune about, "Mr. Tom Moore" while working.]

Lightnin' Hopkins

Singing about Mr. Tom Moore's Farm
[Lyrics]

You know there ain't but one thing,
you know the black man done wrong. [Repeat]
You know there ain't but one thing,
you know this black man done wrong.
I moved my wife and family down

On Mr. Tim Moore's farm.
He sees you by the graveyard,
say I'll save you time getting' in.
You know soon in the morning,
he'll give you scrambled eggs.
Yes, he's liable to call you so soon
you'll catch a mule by his hind legs.
You know I got a telegram this morning.
It say your wife is dead.
I showed it to Mr. Moore,
he says, 'go ahead, nigger,
you know you gotta plow a ridge.'
That white man said,

it's been rainin'.
Yes sir. I'm way behind,
I may let you bury your woman on your dinner time.'
I told him, 'no Mr. Moore, somebody's got to go.
He said, 'if you ain't goin to plow,
get up there and grab your hoe.
This is the life on the farm of Mr. Tom Moore.

THE END

Part 3

OSCAR BROWN JR
IN MEMORIAM: YOUR SPIRIT AND MUSIC LIVE

Jazz in the Valley Concert
Producer: Greer Smith
Musician: Oscar Brown, Jr., vocalist/storyteller; Jimmy Heath; composer/arranger, tenor saxophone; Ray Mantilla, Africanpercussions; K.J. Denhert, guitar/vocal.
Location: West Park Wine Cellar
West Park-on-Hudson, NY
August 29, 2004

Oscar Brown, Jr.Born October 10, 1928 made his transition on May 29, 2005. He was born and raised in Chicago to a middle class that prided itself on its black consciousness to the point where his father wanted to make Texas a separate parent nation state for people of African ancestry. During this time, the oppression for African people of the Americas ran very deep. It was written within this environment we must examine how he became one of the most distinguished and prolific advocate of Black popular Culture.

Little did we know, OSCAR BROWN, JR. was on his last sojourn that in that effort made his last appearance in New York State on August 29, 2004 at the Jazz in the Valley's fifth annual concert held at the winery in West Park, New York. We are simultaneously happy to have experience his gifts at Jazz in the Valley and sadden by his transition to the spirit world of our ancestors of tomorrow world.

The sadness must turn into joy as we celebrate him at this sixth annual Jazz in the Valley Concert. This year we are located in a new ad different venue at this beautiful resort at Williams Lake and conference center. This venue offers an ideal location for loving people who love to enjoy music and leisure activity all within the same breath. In honor of Oscar Brown, Jr. Jazz in the Valley dedicates this issue of our playbill to him. In so doing, this issue will celebrate him by giving our aficionados a different look at our distinguished honoree.

This piece will look at Oscar Brown, Jr. and his impact in the emergence of a new Black Aesthetic. It was during the 1960's C. E. that the high energy reached its intellectual peak in the creation of a new Black thought called the Black Arts Movement. The Black Arts Movement was not a person although a person, Amiri Baraka, is credited wit coining the Movements name. In fact thousands of intellectuals and artists souls of both genders participated in ita development. Many of the major players of the movement have been and are being mentioned elsewhere and deservedly so. Most have not, or when mentioned, never with the notion of pointing out their intellectual acumen and great desire to see Black Art recognized as the world-class phenomenon it is.

What is the intent of this discourse?

This discourse is devoted to OSCAR BROWN JR because even for him this is one aspect that has not received the attention it deserves. This is unfortunate because he was at once a scholar/intellectual and an artist.He naturally felt comfort in both areas. This comfort allowed him to entertain and inform his audiences in the same breath no lectures were required here. This piece will address this intellectual and scholarly aspect of his performance and what he contributed to this development of a new Black Aesthetic.

136

What is the Black Aesthetic?

For this piece, Black Aesthetics mat be defined as the intuitive and philosophical recognition of that constitutes a work of Art (inclusive), ass invented under and within the realm of Black Popular Culture. Black Popular Culture is a process of social intercourse that allows its audience to critique the value of the Art as a subjectively arrived at process. That Art, in this case music, is by performance standards an emotive intellectual intuitively pleasing piece,

How does this occur?

As a founding member who established the governing principles for the study and practice of the Black Arts, Oscar Brown Jr. set the aesthetic rules for Music, Painting, Sculpture, Dance, Theatre, Rhyme, Rhetoric, Story Telling, and the Letters or what we may call the Humanities. He truly can be called a Renaissance product. In other words he can be called Professor or Doctor Brown.Put differently, Dr. Brown should thought of as one of the protector of the Muse. His creative labor set the standard and tone for how the new the new Black Aesthetic would be viewed. It has been through my exposure to Artists such as Oscar Brown, Jr. that has permitted me to understand that there is the Aesthetic of Black Art and how that esthetic process operates.

Stated another way, Professor Brown is the epitome of what Art is when produced when produced and performed by him and his company. To use a cliché where it fits Oscar Brown, Jr. is one of a kind in the most creative use of he word.Let us recall, he is one of the authors of the movement to declare Black Art has a recognizable form of distinction that has its own rules of what Art is. He helped establish the rules by using the Performance Art to demonstrate what constitute Black Art. According to Professor Brown, the artistic beauty, brilliance, genius of creative labor, originality, and/or inventiveness with purposeful intention is when Art comes alive. Aesthetics is the philosophical explanation that provides the backbone for the process an Aficionado uses to engage the performance in Black Creative Music as a listener/observer.

As a supplier of what we should expect to see when we enjoy Black Creative Music – common ally referred to as Jazz- Professor Brown established as creatively workable framework of how we ought to view Black Creative Music. It is through his model that we see Jazz as the creative off-spring of Blues. It is through the improvisation of this Black Creative adventure that we may follow the development of the Aesthetic premise surrounding it. The assumption is that the position and location of Black Creative Music has assumed a "world Music status. This in itself tells us that there is an Aesthetic premise governing its performance. Thus the creative energy of the artistsexposed by the musician allows the love of the songs to ring thru honestly. It is the love that reveals how important the Blues Aesthetic is to governing how we feel. That is the gift Oscar Brown Jr. gave to the Black Arts.

JANN PARKER LIVE AT THE SCHOMBURG LIBRARY FOR THE STUDY OF BLACK LIFE AND CULTURE a liner note that was never published. TransArt, Inc.

Delridge La Veon Hunter

Before I begin this liner note, I must say to you the reader, you must listen to this live recording of Ms Jann Parker. It is truly as collectors item.

Jann Parker is a part of a continuum that has contributed to the aesthetic development of America's art music often called jazz. Right out of the Africans American experience in the United States, this music owes it origin to the dual musical forms that landed on the shores from Africa around four hundred years ago.

These musical forms are referred to as gospel and blues today. During slavery they referred to as "spi'-chuls" and "Devil music." We now know Devil music as blues. Original to the African American, Jazz is the modern 20th century offspring of blues.

Jazz requires a performer to show a unique sound and voicing ability to ever become acceptable as possessing "her own style." Jann Parker possesses both.

As I have watched Jann Parker in performance over the years I have seen her grow and develop as a musician who employs her voicing as a complement to other instruments. I have also watched her develop her own unique style of "carrying a tune." And carry a tune she can. Opening with "I Hear Music" the Octet, led by Aaron Graves, piano, sets a nice upbeat modern swing tempo that offers a harmonic blend that compliments Jann Parker with extreme sensitivity. Entering at the right moment, she approaches the song with a touch that compliments the octet only the way she can. In return the ensemble is set for the live recording. From "I Hear Music" until the end of the session, the octet gives us the treat of our musically entertaining lives.

This obvious life of the sound sends Jann Parker to other levels of performance as they move smoothly into Jazz spiritual of "My Favorite Things." The whole place is alive. The music, the performer, the ensemble, the audience, the theatre and the recording are all live at the Schomburg. From "My Favorite Things" to Mr. Boe Tie" in a bossa nova swing that is suave, funky, and rhythmic the place is jumping. "Mr. Boe Tie" is followed by a clear, with no clutter, swinging blues, of "Spring is Here." With the "I lie in my room" we hear the dynamic use of language. The audience sits in awe as Jann Parker brings us through the lyrics with a true feeling of spring in the air.

With a change of venue we now hear Clifford Brown's "Cherokee" lyrics sung by Jann Parker and solo by James Stewart on tenor saxophone. The tune is swinging upbeat movement in a simulated "cut time" that offers a virtual reality to the real thing. The version Ms. Parker sings is very distinct and obviously her own.

With a quick change of mood vocalist "slides" into a very funky-groove, This little ditty "You Made Your Move Too Soon" is a classic blues that allows the audience join in on the session. Anybody who has seen a Jann Parker performance knows this tune. And, of course, everybody responds by singing, just at the right moment, "You made your move too soon" with a big laughter followed by a thunderous applauds after the tune ends. There obviously is great delight at what is happening this evening at the Schomburg on the first day of Spring, 2004.

After a brief pause, the artist gets the audience's attention by telling everybody what she is about to do next. It's Nina Simone. When she announces to her audience that this is a medley of Nina Simone favorites the audience is mesmerized, indicating a total absorption, by the silence you can feel. The silence is in awe of the occasion. Most are here "dressed up." Beginning with "love me or leave me" Jann sets the tone for what is to come. After "I Love You Porgy," Jann tells the audience about "Sophonia" "Aunt Sady" and "They call me Peaches." This rendition is riveting, gripping, dynamic with a textual interplay of a storyteller. The energy is so compelling that it penetrates the core of this classic Simone composition. Jann Parker is on stage not in a recording studio and everyone can tell.

For a brief moment, I stop to ask my self, "can this be topped?" Only to hear one of the most original renditions of "Caravan" that I have heard. With erotic touches of Africanisms layered throughout "Caravan," many now begin to move their bodies, stomp their feet, clap their hands and groove to a swing with excellent harmony that offers just enough funk to remind me of the Flamenco club in Brooklyn. The groove is infected with a solo by trumpeter, Carlos Francis followed by a piano solo by Aaron Graves that gives us a bar room swing that intensifies the groove.

The high-energy upbeat, funky groove is now mellowed with a ballad composed by Jann Parker's producer Cris White. Entitled, "My Life." the ballad is performed by a duo of piano and vocal. It is a true love story that is beautifully rendered. Aaron Graves is his usual self as he provides just enough feeling to render this a beautiful composition. As Jann Parker voices "Your love has made me strong" you can feel the audience's response. Sentimentality consumes everyone who is within an earshot of this love song. What better way to segue[sp] into the past than with a classic made popular by the Spinners, an R&B group of renown, rendition of "A Mighty Love" arranged by Cris White. Again magnificence is on display as Jann Parker shows why she is such a musical gift. A strong ending gives "A Mighty Love" the classic position it will always hold in the annals of popular culture.

Winding down this very special occasion, Billy Strayhorn's "Three Plus One" gives us, the aficionados, a chance to hear from those other instruments that have beening occuping the horn section while placed on their respective holders all evening. With Strayhorn's seldom performed creative work acting as the artistic work before the Finale "Trying Times Blues," we hear the soprano saxophone, the frugal horn, bass clarinet like playing along with Jann Parker. is simply exquisite.

Bringing the aficionados back to reality, Mr. Parker treats us with a social commentary whose ancestry according Professor Kabwasa, can be traced back, to an old blues form called en-gung by the Mburun people who live in Bndundu Province, Congo. Made popular in the United States during the enslavement of the people from Africa, as the risky secular music of the enslaved Africans, this music has been christened timeless. It is also the base of world beat by Jann who gives the listening audience in the 21st a 20th urban version of what this can sound like when you know what you are doing. This is what is happening while "I sit in on a live recording of Jann Parker at the Schomburg." WOW!

Bibliography

References 1

Abate, Ezra. 2009. Ethiopian Kinit (Scales) Analysis of the formation and structure of the Ethiopian scale system In: Proceedings of the 16th International Conference of Ethiopian Studies, ed. by Svein Ege, Harald Aspen, Birhanu Teferra and Shiferaw Bekele, Trondheim 2009.

Alinsky, Saul, Twelve (12) rules for Radicals.

Butler, Octavia E. 1979. Kindred. Boston: Bea0con.

Chase-Riboud, Baraba.1979. Sally Hemings. (A Novel). Chicago: Chicago Review Press 2009.

Cox, Oliver Cromwell, 1970 Caste, Class, and Race: A Study in Social Dynamics. New York: Monthly Review Press.

Craig, William James. (Editor) 1916. The Complete Works of William Shakespeare. (Arranged by Henry M. Piironen).

De Tocquevilie, Alexis..(Trans Henry Reeve). Democracy in America.

Du Bois, W.E.B.1909. The Souls of Black Folk. New York: Dover Publications, Inc,

_____. 1896. The Suppression of the African Slave Trade to the United States 1638-1870. New York Longmans, Greek, and Co.

Dunbar-Ortiz, Roxanne. An Indigenous Peoples History of the United States. ReVisioning America History.

Engels,Fredrich. 1888. The Communist Manifesto [English edition, edited by Fredrich Engels]

Fanon, Franc [trans. Richard Philcox]. 1967. Black Skin White Masks. New York: Grove Press.

_____. 1963. The Wretched of the Earth. New York: Drove Press.

Fazal, Tanisha M. 2007. State Death: The Politics and Geography of Conquest, Occupation, and Annexation. Princeton: Princeton University Press.

Handsberry, Loraine. 1958. A Raison in three Sun.New York: Random House

Henry, Winston, 1973. Strategy for a Black Agenda. New York: International Publishers.

James, C.L.R. 1963. The Black Jacobins. Vintage Books.

Kwame, Nkrumah. Neo-Colonialism, the Last Stage of Imperialism. ISBN-13: 978-0717801404. ISBN-10: 0717801403

Lynch, Willie. The Willie Lynch Letter and the Making of a Slave.[A Fiction]

Marx, Karl. Das Capital.

Machivelli, Niccolo. 1469-1527. 1982. The Prince. Dover Publications, Inc.

Myrdal Gunnar.1944. An American Dilemma, Harper Books.

Northup. Solomon. 1854. Twelve Years A Slave. Auburn: Derby and Miller.

Orwell, George. 1945. Animal Farm. New York: Harcourt.

Orwell, George. 1949. 1964. New York: Harcourt.

Rodney, Walter, 1972 (2011. How Europe Underdeveloped Africa.

Baltimore: Black Classic Press

Silman, IM Jerry. 1998. The Complete Book of Chess Strategy:

Grandmaster Techniques from A to Z. Los Angeles: Siles Press.

Smith, Adam. 2015. An Inquiry into the Nature and Causes of the Wealth of Nations. Irvine, CA: Xist Publishing.

Sunzi.

Spencer-Brown, G., 1979. Laws of Form.

Stowe, Harriet Beecher. Uncle Tom's Cabin or Life Among The Lowly. A Public Domain Book.

Wagner, Sally. 2001. Roesch. Sisters in Spirit: Haudeenosaunee (Iroquois) Influence on Early AmericanFeminists. Summertown, Inn: Native Voices.

Williams, Eric. 1844 (2015). Capitalism and lavery. Philadelphia: The Great Library Collection.

Woodson, Carter Godwin. 2010. The Mis-Education of the Negro. Seven Treasures Publications.

Reference 2

A Blues Aesthetic. Extracts from 'Modern Tones' by Paul Gilroy and 'Re/Birth of a Nation' by Richard J. Powell Rhapsodies in Black: Art of the Harlem Renaissance (London/California: Hayward Gallery, Institute of International Visual Arts and University of California Press, 1997).

Adorno, Theodor, the Aesthetic Theory, Minneapolis, MN: University of Minnesota Press, 1997.

Adorno, Theodor, The Culture Industry, London: Routledge, 1991.

Baker, Barbara A. The Blues Aesthetic and the Making of American Identity in the Literature of the South. New York: Peter Lang. Modern American Literature. Volume 38, 2003.

Baraka, Amiri. "The 'Blues Aesthetics' And the 'Black Aesthetics': Aesthetics as the Continuing Political History of a Culture," Black Music Research Journal . Vol.11, No. 2, Autumn, 1991.

Born in Slavery: Slave Narratives from the Federal Writers Project, 1936-1937: Washington, D.C. Library of Congress.

Brown, Sterling A. "The Blues as FolkPoetry." .O' Maelly, RobertG . Ed. The Jazz Cadence of American Culture. New York: Columbia University Press.530-551, 1998.

Chilton. John. Sidney Bechet: The Wizard of Jazz. London: The Manchester Free Press,1987.

Evans, Bill. " ImprovisationinJazz." O' Maelly, RobertG . Ed. 1998. The Jazz Cadence of American Culture. New York: Columbia University Press. 269-270. 1998.

Foster, Hal, Editor's Introduction, the Anti-Aesthetic, New York: The New Press, 1998.

Harris, James, Treatise the Second: Discourse on Music, Painting and Poetry, London, 1744.

Harrison-Kahan, Lon. "Structure Would Equal Meaning": Blues and Jazz Aesthetics in the Fiction of Nella Larsen. Tulsa Studies in Women's Literature, Volume 28, Number 2, Fall , pp. 267-289, 2009 . (Article)

Hume , David,An Enquiry Concerning Human Understanding. 1748

Hunter, Delridge L., The Jazz Worker: A Time of Crisis, 1980-1994, Dissertation, Cincinnati, OH: The Union Institute and University. 1995.

_____,The Lyric Poet: A Blues Continuum. Brooklyn, NY: Caribbean Diaspora Press. 2001,

_____, The Invention of the Negro: A Polity of Culture, West Park, NY: Trans Art, INC. Publishing, 2003.

_____, The Position Theory, West Park, NY: TransArt, Inc., 2003.

_____, "Sorrow Songs," Florida International University, African New World Studies International Conference on the Encyclopedia of the African Diaspora, May, 2005.Held at Florida Memorial University, Miami, Florida, 2005.

_____, ,"Blues Aesthetics: A Polity of Culture" (A Position Theory), International Conference on Politics [AND/IN] Aesthetics 4-9 June 2005 - Thessaloniki, Greece & Veliko Turnovo, Bulgaria School of English, Aristotle University of Thessaloniki, Greece Department of English and American Studies, University of Veliko Turnovo, Bulgaria, 2005.

Harrison-Kahan, Lon. "Structure Would Equal Meaning": Blues and Jazz Aesthetics in the Fiction of Nella Larsen, pp. 267-289,2009.

Kant, Immanuel, Critique On Aesthetic Judgment (Part I). Electronic Text Center, University of Virginia Library, 1790.

Kofsky, Frank.. John Coltraneand the Revolution of the 1960's. New York: Pathfinder. 1998.

Matherne, Bobby, "Book Review: Laws of Form by G. Spencer-Brown", Julian Press, New York, 1972, A Reader's Journal---Journey into Understanding, Vol. 1, Good Mountain Press Online Literary Reviews, 1999, Moses, Cat. "The Blues in Toni Morrison's The Bluest Eye." African American Review. 33, 4, 653-637, 1999.

Murray, Albert. The Blue Devils of Nana: a Contemporary American Approach to Aesthetic Statement. New York: De Capo Press, 1997.

_____.Stomping the Blues. NY: De Capo Press, 2000.

_____. Improvisation and the Creative Process."

O' Maelly, RobertG . Ed. 1998. The Jazz Cadence of American Culture. New York: Columbia University Press.111-113, 1998.

O' Maelly, RobertG . Ed. The Jazz Cadence of American Culture. New York: Columbia University Press, 1998.

Powell, Richard J., "Art History and Black Memory: Toward a 'Blues Aesthetic.'"

_____.The Blues Aesthetic: Black Culture and Modernism , Washington, D.C.: Washington Project for the Arts, 1989.

Price, Charles Gower. Got My Own World to Look Through: Jimi Hendrix and the Blues Aesthetic. Journal of American & Comparative Cultures. September 2002. Volume 25, Issue 3-4, Pages 243–478, Volume 25, Issue 3-4, Pages 243–478.

RUDINOW, JOEL. Soul Music: Tracking the Spiritual Roots of Pop from Plato to Motown. The University of Michigan Press. pp. 264, 2010.

Schuiller, Friedrich. 1794-5. On the Aesthetic Education of Man, in a series of letters. Translated by Elizabeth M. Wilkinson and L.A. Willoughby. Oxford: Oxford University Press, 1967.

Schuller, Gunther. Musing:the musical worldofGunther Schuller. Oxford: Oxford University Press, 1986.

Snead, James A."Repetition as a Figure ofBlack Culture." RobertG.O' Meally, Ed. The Jazz Cadence of American Culture. New York: Columbia University Press. 62-81, 1998.

Spencer-Brown, George, Laws of Form. London: New York: E.P. Dutton. 1977.

STEWART, ZAN. The Blues Aesthetic' Exhibit Opens Sunday; Bon Appetit Books Monk Winner Bill Cunliffe. Los Angels Times. Jazz Notes. January 10, 1990.

THE BLUES AESTHETIC: BLACK CULTURE AND MODERNISM. Washington Project for the Arts. Sept. 14-Dec. 9, 1989.

Tolson, Nancy D."Brutal Honesty and Metaphorical Grace": The Blues Aesthetic in Black Children's Literature. Children's Literature Association Quarterly, Volume 25, Number 1, Spring 2000, pp. 56-60 (Article)

Troubadour. Online Encyclopedia, 2009.

Wilson, Olly. "Black Music as an Art Form." RobertG.O' Meally, Ed. The Jazz Cadence of American Culture. New York: Columbia University Press. 82-101, 1998.

DISCOGRAPHY

Count Basie

From Wikipedia, the free encyclopedia

Count Basie Sextet (1954, Clef)

- Count Basie and the Kansas City 7 (1962, Impulse!)

- Basie Swingin' Voices Singin' (1966, EMI)

- Loose Walk (with Roy Eldridge) (1972, Pablo)

- Basie Jam (1973, Pablo)

- The Bosses (with Big Joe Turner) (1973)

- For the First Time (1974, Pablo)

- Satch and Josh (with Oscar Peterson)

- Basie & Zoot (with Zoot Sims) (1975, Pablo)

- For the Second Time (1975, Pablo)

- Basie Jam 2 (1976, Pablo)
- Basie Jam 3 (1976, Pablo)
- Kansas City 5 (1977, Pablo)
- The Gifted Ones (with Dizzy Gillespie) (1977, Pablo)
- Basie Jam: Montreux '77 (live) (1977, Pablo)
- Satch and Josh...Again (with Oscar Peterson) (1977, Pablo)
- Night Rider (with Oscar Peterson) (1978, Pablo)
- Count Basie Meets Oscar Peterson – The Timekeepers (with Oscar Peterson) (1978, Pablo)
- Yessir, That's My Baby (with Oscar Peterson) (1978, Pablo)
- Kansas City 8: Get Together (1979, Pablo)
- Kansas City 7 (1980, Pablo)
- Kansas City 6 (1981, Pablo)
- Mostly Blues...and Some Others(1983, Pablo)

JOHN COLTRANE

Impulse!

1961:

- Africa/Brass
- The Complete 1961 Village Vanguard Recordings (1961) (4 discs)
- 1962:
- Ballads
- Coltrane
- Duke Ellington & John Coltrane
- 1963:
- John Coltrane and Johnny Hartman
- Impressions
- Live at Birdland
- Newport '63

- 1964:
- Crescent
- A Love Supreme (RIAA: Gold)
- 1965:
- Ascension
- First Meditations
- Gleanings
- Infinity
- The John Coltrane Quartet Plays
- Kulu Sé Mama
- Live at the Half Note: One Up, One Down
- Live in Seattle
- Living Space
- The Major Works of John Coltrane
- Meditations
- Om
- To the Beat of a Different Drum
- Transition
- Selflessness: Featuring My Favorite Things
- Sun Ship
- New Thing at Newport [Coltrane on one side, Archie Shepp on the other]

MILES DAVIS

COLUMBIA RECORDS

'Round About Midnight

- Released: March 18, 1957
- Recorded: October 27, 1955 – June 5, 1956
- Label: Columbia

Format: LP

Miles Ahead

- Released: 1957
- Recorded: May 6, 1957 – August 22, 1957
- Label: Columbia
- Format: LP

Milestones

- Released: 1958
- Recorded: April 2, 1958 – April 3, 1958
- Label: Columbia
- Format: LP

Porgy and Bess

- Released: 1958
- Recorded: July 22, 1958 – August 18, 1958
- Label: Columbia
- Format: LP

1958 Miles

- Released: 1958
- Recorded: May 26, 1958
- Label: Columbia
- Format: LP

Kind of Blue

- Released: August 17, 1959
- Recorded: March 2, 1959 – April 22, 1959
- Label: Columbia

Format: LP, Reel Tape

Sketches of Spain

- Released: July 18, 1960
- Recorded: November 15, 1959 – November 20, 1959
- Label: Columbia

Format: LP, Reel Tape

Someday My Prince Will Come

- Released: December 11, 1961
- Recorded: March 7, 1961 – March 21, 1961
- Label: Columbia

Format: LP

Quiet Nights(with Gil Evans)

- Released: December 1963
- Recorded: July 27, 1962 – April 17, 1963
- Label: Columbia

Format: LP, Reel Tape

Seven Steps to Heaven

- Released: 1963
- Recorded: April 16, 1963 – May 14, 1963
- Label: Columbia
- Format: LP, Reel Tape

E.S.P.

- Released: November 1965
- Recorded: January 20, 1965 – January 22, 1965
- Label: Columbia

Format: LP

Sorcerer

- Released: 1967
- Recorded: August 21, 1962 – May 24, 1967
- Label: Columbia

Format: LP

Nefertiti

- Released: 1968
- Recorded: June 7, 1967 – July 19, 1967
- Label: Columbia

Format: LP

Miles in the Sky

- Released: 1968
- Recorded: January 16, 1968 – May 17, 1968
- Label: Columbia

Format: LP

Filles de Kilimanjaro

- Released: January 29, 1969
- Recorded: June 19, 1968 – September 24, 1968
- Label: Columbia

Format: LP, Reel Tape

In a Silent Way

- Released: July 30, 1969
- Recorded: February 18, 1969
- Label: Columbia

Format: LP

Bitches Brew

- Released: April 1970
- Recorded: August 19, 1969 – January 28, 1970
- Label: Columbia

Format: LP, Reel Tape

A Tribute to Jack Johnson

- Released: February 24, 1971
- Recorded: February 18 – April 7, 1970
- Label: Columbia
- Format: LP, CD, CS

Live-Evil

- Released: November 17, 1971
- Recorded: February 6, 1970 – December 19, 1970
- Label: Columbia

Format: LP, CD

On the Corner

- Released: October 11, 1972
- Recorded: June 1, 1972 – June 6, 1972
- Label: Columbia
- Format: LP, CD

Big Fun

- Released: April 19, 1974
- Recorded: November 19, 1969 – June 12, 1972
- Label: Columbia

Format: LP, 0CD

Get Up with It

- Released: November 22, 1974
- Recorded: May 19, 1970 – October 7, 1974
- Label: Columbia

Format: CD

Water Babies

- Released: November 2, 1976
- Recorded: June 1967 – November 1968
- Label: Columbia

Format: CD

Kenny Dorham

(From Wikipedia, the free encyclopedia)

As leader

- 1953: Kenny Dorham Quintet (Debut)
- 1955: Afro-Cuban (Blue Note)
- 1956: 'Round About Midnight at the Cafe Bohemia (Blue Note)
- 1957: Jazz Contrasts (Riverside) featuring Sonny Rollins
- 1957: 2 Horns / 2 Rhythm (Riverside) featuring Ernie Henry
- 1958: This Is the Moment! (Riverside)
- 1959: Blue Spring (Riverside) with Cannonball Adderley
- 1959: Quiet Kenny (New Jazz)
- 1960: The Kenny Dorham Memorial Album (Xanadu)
- 1960: Jazz Contemporary (Time)
- 1960: Show Boat (Time)
- 1961: Whistle Stop (Blue Note)
- 1961: Inta Somethin' (Pacific Jazz)
- 1962: Matador (United Artists)
- 1963: Una Mas (Blue Note)

- 1963: Scandia Skies (Steeple Chase)
- 1963: Short Story (Steeple Chase)
- 1964: Trompeta Toccata (Blue Note)

Duke Ellington
(From Wikipedia, the free encyclopedia)

Compilations

- Complete Works: 1924-1947 (Proper UK) (2003) (40 discs)
- The Centennial Edition: The Complete RCA-Victor Recordings (1999) (24 discs)
- The Complete RCA-Victor Mid-Forties Recordings (2000)
- The Private Collection (1956–1971) (Saja) (10 discs)
- The Duke Box (Storyville) (2007) (8 discs)
- 1936-40 Small Group Sessions (Mosaic) (7 discs)
- The Complete Capitol Recordings (Blue Note) (1999) (5 discs)
- The Reprise Studio Recordings (Mosaic) (5 discs)
- Early Ellington: The Complete Brunswick And Vocalion Recordings Of
- Duke Ellington, 1926-1931 (GRP Records/ Verve Music Group) (3 discs)
- Masterpieces, 1926-1949 (Proper) (4 discs)
- The Gold Collection, 40 Classic Performances (Proper/Retro) (2 discs)
- Duke Ellington's Incidental Music for Shakespeare's Play Timon of Athens, adapted by Stanley Silverman (1993). Ellington does not perform on this recording, but it includes previously unreleased compositions.

Charlie Parker

1949

- Charlie Parker - Broadcast Performances, Vol. 2 (ESP)
- The Metronome All Stars - From Swing To Be-Bop (RCA Camden)
- Jazz At The Philharmonic - J.A.T.P. At Carnegie Hall 1949 (Pablo)
- Rara Avis Avis, Rare Bird (Stash)
- Various Artists - Alto Saxes (Norgran)

- Bird On The Road (Jazz Showcase)

- Charlie Parker/Dizzy Gillespie - Bird And Diz (Universal (Japan))

- Charlie Parker - Bird In Paris (Bird in Paris)

- Charlie Parker In France 1949 (Jazz O.P. (France))

- Charlie Parker - Bird Box, Vol. 2 (Jazz Up (Italy))

- Bird's Eyes, Vol. 5 (Philology)

- Charlie Parker with Strings (Clef)

- Bird's Eyes, Vol. 2 (Philology)

- Bird's Eyes, Vol. 3 (Philology)

- Dance Of The Infidels (S.C.A.M.)

Sonny Rollins

1975	Nucleus	Milestone
1976	The Way I Feel	Milestone
1977	Easy Living	Milestone
1978	Don't Stop the Carnival	Milestone
1979	Don't Ask	Milestone
1980	Love at First Sight	Milestone
1981	No Problem	Milestone
1982	Reel Life	Milestone
1984	Sunny Days, Starry Nights	Milestone
1985	The Solo Album	Milestone
1986	G-Man	Milestone
1987	Dancing in the Dark	Milestone
1989	Falling in Love with Jazz	Milestone
1991	Here's to the People	Milestone
1993	Old Flames	Milestone
1996	Sonny Rollins + 3	Milestone
1998	Global Warming	Milestone
2000	This Is What I Do	Milestone
2001	Without a Song: The 9/11 Concert	Milestone
2006	Sonny, Please	Emarcy

Bibliography/References 2

Abate1 Ezra. "Ethiopian Kiñit (scales) Analysis of the formation and structure of the Ethiopian scale system." Proceedings of the 16th International Conference of Ethiopian Studies, ed. by Svein Ege, Harald Aspen, Birhanu Teferra and Shiferaw Bekele, Trondheim 2009.

P.1213

Adorno, Theodor, 1997, the Aesthetic Theory, Minneapolis, MN: University of Minnesota Press.

Adorno, Theodor, 1991, the Culture Industry, London: Routledge.

Albertson, Chris. 1982. Bessie. New York: Stein & Day.

Alderman, Kimberly L. "Slave Artists As Powerful Reality Creators: Taking Responsibility and Rejecting Race Consciousness."Thurgood Marshall Law Review, Vol. 33, No. 1, 2008. 1-32.

Allen, William Francis, el al. 1867. Slave Songs in the United States. New York: A. Simpson.

Baker, Barbara A.2003.The Blues Aesthetic and the Making of American Identity in the Literature of the South. New York: Peter Lang. Modern American Literature. Volume 38.

Baraka, Amiri. "The `Blues Aesthetics' And the `Black Aesthetics': Aesthetics as the

Continuing Political History of a Culture," Black Music Research Journal .

Vol.11, No. 2, Autumn, 1991.

Bebey, Francis. 1975. African Music: A People's Art. Westport: Lawrence Hill & Co

Born in Slavery: Slave Narratives from the Federal Writers Project, 1936-1937: Washington, D.C. Library of Congress.

Brown, Sterling A. "The Blues as FolkPoetry." .O' Maelly, RobertG . Ed. 1998. The Jazz Cadence of American Culture. New York: Columbia University Press.530-551.

Cavalli-Sforza, L. Luca, Paolo Menozzi, and Alberto Piazza. 1994. The History and Geography of the Human Genes. Princeton, N J: Princeton University Press.

Charters, Samuel. 1992. Po' Lightnin'. New York: Muse Records. 7PCD-4406-2

Chilton. John. 1987. Sidney Bechet: The Wizard of Jazz. London: The Manchester Free Press.

_____. 1981. The Roots of the Blues: An African Search.

New York: A Perigee Book.

Chernoff, John Miller. 1979. African Rhythm and African Sensibility. Chicago: The University of Chicago Press.

Collier, James Lincoln. 1985. Louis Armstrong: A Biography. London: Pan Books.

Costello, Mark and David Foster Wallace. 1990. Signifying Rappers: Rap and Race in the Urban Present. New York: The Ecco Press.

Courlander, Harold. 1996. A Treasury of African Folklore.New York:Marlowe & Company.

_____. 1976. ATreasury of Afro-American folklore. New York: Crown Publishers.

Courlander, Harold. 1963. Negro Folk Music, U.S.A. New York: Columbia University Press.

50

Cunard, Nancy, Ed. 1970. Negro: An Anthology. New York: Frederick Ungar Publishing Co.

Dixon, Willie - I Am The Blues [Live Full DVD] 50:44

Dietz, Betty Warner and Michael Babatunde Olatunji. 1965. Musical Instruments of Africa: Their Nature, Use, and Place in the Land of a Deeply Musical People. New York: The John Day Company

Du Bois, W.E.B. 1982 (1903). The Souls of Black Folk. New York: A Signet Classic.

_____ 1909. John Brown, Philadelphia: George W. Jacobs & Company.

Dunbar, Paul Laurence. 1913. The Complete Poems of Paul Laurence Dunbar. New York: Dobb, Mead & Company.

_____. 1992. The Life & Works of Paul Laurence Dunbar. Nashville: Winston-Derek Publishers, Inc.

Ely, Don. Georgia" Thomas A. Dorsey The Star Gennett Foundation, Inc. Rochester, Michigan.

Epstein, Dena J. 1977. Sinful Tunes and Spirituals: Black Folk Music to the Civil War. Champaign: University of Illinois Press.

Evans, Bill. " Improvisationinjazz." O' Maelly, RobertG . Ed. 1998. The Jazz Cadence of American Culture. New York: Columbia University Press. 269-270. 1998.

Ferris, William. 1978. Blues From The Delta. New York: Da Capo Press.[Intro. by Billy Taylor, 1984 copyright]

Finn, Julio, 1991. The Bluesman: The Musical Heritage of Blackmen and Women in the Americas. New York: Interlink Books.

Fisher, Miles Mark. 1990. Negro Slave Songs in the United States.

New York: A Citadel Press Book.

Foster, Hal, 1998, Editor's Introduction, the Anti-Aesthetic, New York: The New Press.

Gellert, Lawrence. ED. 1938. Negro Slave Songs of Protest. New York: Carl Fisher,

Harris, Michael W. 1992. The Rise of Gospel Blues: The Music of Thomas Andrew Dorsey in The Urban Church. New York: Oxford University Press.

Handy, W.C. 1969. Father of The Blues: An Autobiography. New York: Da Capo Press.

Harris, James, 1744. Treatise the Second: Discourse on Music, Painting and Poetry, London.

Hume , David.An Enquiry Concerning Human Understanding.

Hunter, Delridge L. "Interview with Gerry Eastman," Cultural Streams, New York: WNYE T.V., May 2, 1992. Gerry Eastman is a bassist, guitarist, composer, arranger, producer, educator, and Mr. Eastman producers and records his orchestra for the Williamsburg Music Center's recorded label. Of which he is the executive director/founder of.

_____. 1995, The Jazz Worker: A Time of Crisis, 1980-1994, Dissertation, Cincinnati, OH: The Union Institute and University.

_____, 2001, The Lyric Poet: A Blues Continuum. Brooklyn, NY: Caribbean Diaspora Press.

_____, 2003, The Invention of the Negro: A Polity of Culture, West Park, NY: TransArt INC. Publishing.

_____, 2003, The Position Theory, West Park, NY: TransArt, Inc.

_____. 2005, "Sorrow Songs," Florida International University, African New World Studies International Conference on the Encyclopedia of the African Diaspora, May, 2005.Held at Florida Memorial University, Miami, Florida

_____, 2005,"Blues Aesthetics: A Polity of Culture" (A Position Theory), International Conference on Politics [AND/IN] Aesthetics 4-9 June 2005 - Thessaloniki, Greece & Veliko Turnovo, Bulgaria School of English, Aristotle University of Thessaloniki, Greece Department of English and American Studies, University of Veliko Turnovo, Bulgaria.

Kant, Immanuel . 1790. Critique On Aesthetic Judgment (Part I). Electronic Text Center, University of Virginia Library

Professor Kabwasa, Bndundu Province, Congo, Distinguished Professor. Toledo University, Ohio, February 15, 2000

Kofsky, Frank. 1998. John Coltraneand the Revolution of the 1960's. New York: Pathfinder.

Locke, Alain, 1936, The Negro and His Music-Negro Art: Past and Present, New York: Arno/The New York Times.

Marsh, J. B. T. MDCCCLXXXV. The Story of the Jubilee Singers with their Songs. London: Hodder and Stoughton. [These songs were collected from freed slaves and/or their offspring and arranged by George L. White, and Theodore F. Seward.]{The original Jubilee Song Book.}

Matherne, Bobby, "Book Review: Laws of Form by G. Spencer-Brown", Julian Press, New York, 1972, A Reader's Journal---Journey into Understanding, Vol. 1, 1999, Good Mountain Press Online Literary Reviews.

Murrray, Albert. 1997. The Blue Devils of Nana: a Contemporary American Approach to Aesthetic Statement. New York:

_____.2000. Stomping the Blues. NY: De Capo Press.

_____. Improvisation and the Creative Process."O' Maelly, RobertG . Ed. 1998. The Jazz Cadence of American Culture. New York: Columbia University Press.111-113. 1998.

Oliver, Paul. 1971. Bessie Smith. New York: A.S. Barnes.

O' Maelly, RobertG . Ed. 1998. The Jazz Cadence of American Culture. New York: Columbia University Press.

Palmer, Robert. 1981. Deep Blues. New York: A Penguin Book.

_____. 1996.Criots of West Africa: An Introductory Essay .Ellipsis.Arts. Roslyn, NY

Pike, Gustavus D 1874.The singing campaign for ten thousand pounds; or, The Jubilee singers in Great Britain. London: Hodder and Stroughton:,

Powell, Richard J., "Art History and Black Memory: Toward a 'Blues Aesthetic.'"

RobertG.O' Meally, Ed. The Jazz Cadence of American Culture. New York: Columbia University Press. 182-195. 1998.

Rawick, George P., General Editor. 1972. The American Slave: A Composite Autobiography. Vol I-9.

Schuiller, Friedrich. 1794-5. On the Aesthetic Education of Man, in a series of letters. Translated by Elizabeth M. Wilkinson and L.A. Willoughby. Oxford: Oxford University Press, 1967.

Schuller, Gunther. 1986. Musing:the musical worldofGunther Schuller. Oxford: Oxford University Press.

Snead, James A."Repetition as a Figure ofBlack Culture." RobertG.O' Meally, Ed. The Jazz Cadence of American Culture. New York: Columbia University Press. 62-81. 1998.

Southern, Eileen. 1971. The Music of Black Americans: A History. New York: W.W. Norton & Co.

Spencer-Brown, George, 1977, Laws of Form. London: New York: E.P. Dutton.

Trotter, James M. 1881, Music and some Highly Musical people, Boston: Lee and Shepard, Publishers, New YorkCharles T. Dillingham, 262-263.

Troubadour, 2009, Online Encyclopedia.

We owe people like Wynonie, Harris, Big Joe, Meade lux, Albert Ammonds, Pete Johnson, Elmore James, and the original blues man Robert Johnson for boogie woogie, rockabilly, and rock n roll. These people are the ones Jerry Lee, Elvis, Carl Perkins, Fats Domino, Chuck Berry, Johnny Cash and many others learned from to give us music.

Discography

, Willie Dixon Live"I am the Blues"(Full DVD)

The Miles Davis Quintet Live Walkin'" November 7, 1967 at the Stadthalle Karlsruhe, Germany Miles Davis Ron Carter. Herbie Hancock, Wayne Shorter Tony Williams Jazz

_____. Live"All Blues" November 12, 2964. Milan, Italy. Miles Davis, trumpet, Wayne Shorter, tenor sax, Herbie Hancock - piano Ron Carter - bass Tony Williams – drums

Charles Mingus - Moanin' Mingus Big Band 1993

THELONIOUS MONK - Blue Monk

Thelonious Monk - 'Round Midnight - 1966

Thelonius Monk – "Evidence" (HQ) Straight No Chaser [Cinema]

Thelonius Monk Evidence Bebop Jazz Swing Bass Piano

Big Mama Thornton Sings "Hound Dog"1953

Big Mama Thornton - Ball and Chain (Live)

Robert Johnson- Crossroad

Robert Johnson Movie RARE

Animated Sheet Music: "Giant Steps" by John Coltrane

John Coltrane - Blue train

John Coltrane live "Naima".1965